GENETICS

Problem Solving Guide
Second Edition

William R. Wellnitz

AUGUSTA COLLEGE
Augusta, Georgia

WCB Wm. C. Brown Publishers
Dubuque, Iowa • Melbourne, Australia • Oxford, England

Book Team

Editor *Elizabeth M. Sievers*
Developmental Editor *Robin P. Steffek*
Production Editor *Julie L. Wilde*
Publishing Services Coordinator-Design *Barbara J. Hodgson*
Art Processor *Brenda A. Ernzen*

Wm. C. Brown Publishers
A Division of Wm. C. Brown Communications, Inc.

Vice President and General Manager *Beverly Kolz*
Vice President, Publisher *Kevin Kane*
Vice President, Director of Sales and Marketing *Virginia S. Moffat*
Vice President, Director of Production *Colleen A. Yonda*
National Sales Manager *Douglas J. DiNardo*
Marketing Manager *Patrick E. Reidy*
Advertising Manager *Janelle Keeffer*
Production Editorial Manager *Renée Menne*
Publishing Services Manager *Karen J. Slaght*
Permissions/Records Manager *Connie Allendorf*

Wm. C. Brown Communications, Inc.

President and Chief Executive Officer *G. Franklin Lewis*
Corporate Senior Vice President, President of WCB Manufacturing *Roger Meyer*
Corporate Senior Vice President and Chief Financial Officer *Robert Chesterman*

Cover photo: © Will and Deni McIntyre, Photo Researchers, Inc.

Cover and interior design by Deborah Schneck

A Times Mirror Company

Library of Congress Catalog Card Number: 93–74523

ISBN 0–697–13739–2

Printed in the United States of America by Wm. C. Brown Communications, Inc.,
2460 Kerper Boulevard, Dubuque, IA 52001

10 9 8 7 6 5 4 3

Preface

Genetics is often difficult for the beginning student, partly because it deals with abstract concepts. In performing a genetic analysis, we obtain results in terms of numbers and kinds of progeny, then make inferences about what genotypes must have been present in the parents. These inferences are based on logical deductions and a modicum of rules or concepts.

Unfortunately, the concepts are often lost or obscured in the typical presentation of various topics. What I have strived to do in this manual is to highlight the concept and then show how a given concept can be used to solve a problem.

This manual is meant to supplement, not replace, your text. It assumes that you have been exposed at least once to the topics covered in a given chapter. The nature of the manual is such that detailed descriptions of biological processes cannot be given. You should refer to your text and class notes for such descriptions. The problems presented, although not exhaustive by any means, should provide exposure to almost all the types of problems you will encounter in performing genetic analyses. More detailed problem sets can be found in most current genetic texts.

The second edition of this manual contains a number of changes from the first edition.

1. The number of problems has almost doubled, and the new problems vary in difficulty. The more challenging problems can usually be found at the end of the problem set.
2. More human examples have been scattered throughout many of the chapters in hopes of showing how principles that seem esoteric really apply to humans as well.
3. Two new chapters on population genetics have been added.
4. Chapters 10–12 have been completely rewritten and extensively expanded, partly to reflect the current state of genetics, and partly to clear up confusing areas from the first edition.

An appreciation for and a mastery of genetic principles can only be achieved through the careful working of as many problems as possible. For any problem, begin with a blank sheet of paper, and write down the cross and the progeny, if given. Then determine what is being asked in the problem. Usually you are asked to determine the genetic basis *(genotypes)* for the results or to predict expected progeny *(phenotypes)*.

Each chapter includes the following:

Essential concepts: highlighted in boldface. These concepts typically take the form "A particular result suggests . . . . " Each concept includes a sample problem, a detailed solution, and often supplementary information. Many problems here include a genotype/phenotype key, and most new terms are defined in the text of the explanation.

Chapter summary: key ideas to keep in mind when working genetic problems pertinent to concepts presented in the chapter. These summary statements are general in nature.

Practice problems: collection of problems that incorporates *all* the concepts of the chapter. The concepts used in the problems are not necessarily covered in the order of presentation, and some problems require the use of more than one concept.

Detailed solutions: at the end of the manual. The answer is given first, followed by a detailed explanation of how you should have proceeded. The concepts that you needed to use are identified in the explanations.

In addition, there is a separate chapter entitled **Master Problems.** These problems are meant to be challenging, and often involve concepts from more than one chapter.

Use of the manual:

1. Skim the appropriate chapter, concentrating only on the concepts. Pause to reflect on the concepts, but do not attempt to memorize them.
2. Examine the summary and allow these statements to soak in.
3. Reread the chapter, concentrating this time on the sample problems and their solutions. Try to work the problems without looking at the accompanying solution.
4. Attempt the practice problems. Try to determine which concept(s) is(are) involved in each problem. Always work from simple to complex. Suppose, for example, you are using chapter 2, and see four phenotypes in the progeny. Do the phenotypic ratios most closely resemble a 9:3:3:1, a 3:3:1:1, or a 1:1:1:1 ratio? Depending on the ratio, you can then deduce the genotypes of the parents. When possible, try to begin your solutions by making a key for genotypes and phenotypes.
5. Do not look at the answer until you have struggled with the problem for a while. It is easy to fall into the trap of looking at the answer and assuming that you now know how to solve the problem. You will only master the concepts if you grapple with the problem for a while.

A similar approach can be used in working other genetic problems you encounter. Remember, the more problems you attempt, the clearer the concepts become and the better your understanding of genetics.

Acknowledgments

I am grateful to the many teachers and students who wrote to point out errors or to offer suggestions, and especially to students in my genetics class the past few years for comments on various stages of this book. I do not intend to slight them by omitting their names; they should, however, recognize that many of their comments were incorporated into the second edition. I am also grateful to Thuy Nguyen for carefully working all the problems and checking the text for accuracy. The people at Wm. C. Brown, especially Kevin Kane, Robin Steffek, Julie Wilde, and the production staff, have all been very helpful and patient. Finally, my family, and especially my wife, Dianne, deserves special thanks for enduring my mood swings and periods of isolation from them.

The following reviewers critiqued various parts of the second edition. Henri Roger Maurice, Barat College; David J. Cotter, Georgia College; Peter J. Wejksnora, University of Wisconsin-Milwaukee; Paul Goldstein, University of Texas at El Paso; Margarida Lopes, Queen's University; Ernest R. Vyse, Montana State University. I may not have agreed with all of their comments, but each comment was carefully considered. Errors or misconceptions that remain are my fault.

William R. Wellnitz
Augusta, Georgia, March, 1994

The Author

William R. Wellnitz is an associate professor of biology at Augusta College. He holds a B.S. and a Ph.D. from Cornell University and an M.A. from the University of Colorado. Prior to coming to Augusta College, he taught at Davidson College and was a postdoctoral fellow at Duke University.

Table of Contents

G. The allele frequency of a recessive allele after selection is

$$q_s = q(1 - sq)/(1 - sq^2), \text{ where } s = \text{selection coefficient.}$$

H. If a homozygous recessive genotype is completely lethal, the recessive allele frequency after one generation is $q/(1 + q)$.

I. If the heterozygote has an advantage over both homozygotes, the equilibrium frequency of the recessive allele, $\hat{q}$, should be

$$\frac{s_1}{(s_1 + s_2)}, \text{ where } s_1 = \text{selection coefficient of homozygous dominant and}$$

s_2 = selection coefficient of homozygous recessive.

J. If both mutations and selection are operating, the equilibrium frequency of the recessive allele after selection is approximately $\sqrt{\mu / s}$ and μ/s for a dominant allele.

Single Gene Ratios

A. The presence of only one phenotype in the progeny may suggest one gene.

If both parents are homozygous for the same allele, each parent produces only one type of gamete, and progeny are identical.

$$AA \times AA \quad \text{or} \quad aa \times aa$$
$$\downarrow \qquad\qquad\qquad \downarrow$$
$$\text{all } AA \qquad\qquad \text{all } aa$$

If one parent is homozygous dominant, all progeny receive at least one dominant allele; hence, all progeny show the dominant trait.

$$AA \times aa \qquad\qquad AA \times Aa$$
$$\downarrow \qquad\qquad\qquad\qquad \downarrow$$
$$\text{all } Aa \qquad\qquad \text{½} AA : \text{½} Aa$$
$$\text{(all dominant)} \qquad \text{(all dominant)}$$

EXAMPLE: In *Drosophila*, a cross between a dark-bodied fly and a tan-bodied fly yields all tan-bodied flies. What is the mode of inheritance?

We see two different parents but only one type of progeny. Since the progeny express the dominant trait, let T = tan and t = dark.

The cross must be the following:

$$TT \times tt$$
$$\downarrow$$
$$\text{all } Tt$$
$$\text{(tan)}$$

B. The presence of two phenotypes in the progeny suggests one gene and at least one heterozygous parent.

The two phenotypes can arise when:

1. Both parents are heterozygous:

$$Aa \times Aa$$
$$\downarrow$$
$$\text{¾} A\text{-} \quad : \quad \text{¼} aa$$
$$\text{(dominant)} \quad \text{(recessive)}$$

EXAMPLE: When two black mice are mated, 16 of the progeny are black and five are brown. Diagram the cross.

Since both parents are of the same phenotype, and the progeny are of two phenotypes, both parents must be heterozygous, and black is dominant to brown. Let B = black and b = brown.

$$Bb \times Bb$$
$$\downarrow$$
$$3/4\ B\text{-} : 1/4\ bb$$
$$\text{(black)}\quad\text{(brown)}$$

2. One parent is homozygous recessive and one parent is heterozygous:

$$Aa \times aa$$
$$\downarrow$$
$$1/2\ Aa : 1/2\ aa$$
$$\text{(dominant)}\quad\text{(recessive)}$$

EXAMPLE: A mating between a black mouse and a brown mouse yields eight black and seven brown progeny. Diagram the cross.

We see two phenotypes in equal amounts. One parent must be homozygous and the other heterozygous.

$$Bb \times bb$$
$$\downarrow$$
$$1/2\ Bb : 1/2\ bb$$

We can't tell from this cross alone which allele is dominant. To determine dominance, we need information similar to that in example B-1.

C. A 3:1 ratio in the progeny suggests one gene and both parents heterozygous.

EXAMPLE: Refer again to the cross in example B-1.

$$\text{black} \times \text{black}$$
$$\downarrow$$
$$16 \text{ black} : 5 \text{ brown}$$

Since we see two phenotypes, we probably are dealing with only one gene. In order to get two phenotypes, we must have two alleles present. If black were recessive, the cross would be:

$$bb \times bb,$$

which yields identical progeny (black). This result is not seen. If black is dominant and at least one parent is homozygous, the cross is then $BB \times Bb$, which yields all B- (black), a result not seen. The cross must be:

$$Bb \times Bb$$
$$\downarrow$$
$$3/4\ B\text{-} : 1/4\ bb$$
$$\text{(black)}\quad\text{(brown)}$$

If you see two phenotypes in the progeny, and the ratio approaches 3:1, then both parents are probably heterozygous.

Note: Implicit in this line of reasoning is that both parents have the same phenotype. If both parents have the same phenotype, and a 3:1 ratio is observed, one gene is probable (see section 2-J for exceptions).

D. A 1:1 ratio among progeny suggests one gene and a heterozygote × homozygote.

If you get a 1:1 ratio, look at the parents. If they have different phenotypes, the above situation is probably true. However, you can't determine which allele is dominant merely from this cross; more information is needed.

EXAMPLE: A cross between a tall and a short tomato plant yields 26 tall and 28 short. What are the genotypes of the parents?

We see two phenotypes in approximately equal amounts; we also see that the parents had different phenotypes. Therefore, if T = tall and t = short, the cross is probably:

$$Tt \times tt$$
$$\downarrow$$
$$1/2 \ Tt : 1/2 \ tt$$

E. Three phenotypes among the progeny in a 1:2:1 ratio suggests one gene with incomplete dominance (the heterozygote has a different phenotype than either homozygote).

Before beginning the analysis, look at the phenotypes. Does one seem to be a blend of the other two? If so, you probably have incomplete dominance. Other possibilities involving at least two genes exist, and will be discussed in chapter 2. Always work from the simplest explanation to the more complex; hence, consider one gene first.

EXAMPLE: A plant with red flowers is crossed to a plant with white flowers. All the progeny are pink. When the pink flowers are crossed, 11 red, 23 pink, and 12 white-flowered plants result. What is the mode of inheritance of color?

Pink seems to be a blend of red and white. Assume that red and white are homozygous. If one of the colors were dominant, all the progeny from the first cross should be either red or white. This is not seen; therefore neither color is dominant.

Pink probably represents the heterozygote. Let C = gene for color, C^r = red, and C^w = white. Therefore the first cross can be indicated as:

$$C^rC^r \times C^wC^w$$
$$\text{(red)} \quad \text{(white)}$$
$$\downarrow$$
$$\text{all } C^rC^w$$
$$\text{(pink)}$$

The second cross is:

$$C^rC^w \times C^rC^w$$
$$\text{(pink)} \times \text{(pink)}$$

Any two heterozygotes will always yield a 1:2:1 genotypic ratio, or in this case, $^1/_4$ C^rC^r : $^1/_2 C^rC^w$: $^1/_4 C^wC^w$. Approximately half of the progeny should be pink. We examine the cross and see that $^{23}/_{46}$ are pink.

F. A 2:1 ratio among progeny suggests one gene and a homozygous lethal.

Note that we still have only two phenotypes, and are therefore probably dealing with only one gene. In order for this to be true, both parents must be heterozygous, and thus show the same phenotype. First determine if both parents are identical.

Consider a cross between two heterozygotes:

$$Aa \times Aa$$

This cross always yields the following genotypic ratio:

$^1/_4 AA$: $^1/_2 Aa$: $^1/_4 aa$. Normally Aa and AA have the same phenotype, and we expect a 3:1 ratio. But in this case, one homozygote dies.

If the lethal is counted as a phenotype, there are actually three phenotypes. You can only count the organisms that you see. Among the progeny, not the survivors, $^1/_2$ are expected to be Aa and $^1/_4$ to be aa. Among the survivors, $^2/_3$ are Aa and $^1/_3$ are aa; therefore a 2:1 ratio is seen.

EXAMPLE: In *Drosophila*, two curly-winged flies are mated and produce 50 curly and 23 straight-winged flies. Explain these results by diagramming the cross.

Two phenotypes are present and both parents have the same phenotype. These facts suggest that we are dealing with one gene and that each parent is heterozygous. Normally we would expect a 3:1 ratio. Without performing any statistics, we can see that $^{50}/_{23}$ does not approach 3:1. The ratio is much closer to 2:1. Curly must be dominant to straight, since both parents are curly and because curly represents the majority of the offspring. Therefore, the homozygous curly flies must die before hatching. Let Cy = curly and cy = straight.

$$Cycy \times Cycy$$
$$\downarrow$$
$$^1/_4 \; CyCy : \;^1/_2 \; Cycy : \;^1/_4 \; cycy$$
$$\text{(dead)} \qquad \text{(curly)} \qquad \text{(straight)}$$

G. If identical phenotypes yield different ratios in different crosses, consider the possibility of multiple alleles.

EXAMPLE: In screech owls, crosses between red and silver individuals sometimes yield all red; sometimes $^1/_2$ red : $^1/_2$ silver; and sometimes $^1/_2$ red : $^1/_4$ white : $^1/_4$ silver. Crosses between two reds yield either all red; $^3/_4$ red : $^1/_4$ silver; or $^3/_4$ red : $^1/_4$ white. What is the mode of inheritance?

In each case, we see that all ratios could result from a single gene (3:1, 1:2:1, and 1:1). We can easily explain the red and silver if we assume that red is dominant over silver. Thus, the first cross could be:

$$RR \times rr \text{ or } Rr \times rr$$

Similarly, the second cross could be:

$$RR \times R\text{-} \text{ or } Rr \times Rr$$

But we cannot explain any of the white progeny with only two alleles. Because all the ratios are single gene ratios, we must propose a third allele that produces white when homozygous; red must be dominant to white. Note that a given diploid individual can only have two alleles. To list all possible genotypes and their phenotypes, let R = red, and r = non-red.

RR, Rr^s, Rr^w : red (red is dominant to all other alleles)

$r^s r^s$: silver

$r^w r^w$: white

What can we do with $r^s r^w$? Assume one of them is dominant; in this case, assume s is dominant to w. Therefore $r^s r^w$ = silver.

Now go back to the results. By our model, $r^w r^w$ is white. Therefore, in order to get white progeny, each parent must have at least one w allele to contribute. The cross of red by silver must be:

$$Rr^w \times r^s r^w$$
$$\downarrow$$

$^1/_4 \ Rr^s : {}^1/_4 \ Rr^w : {}^1/_4 \ r^s r^w : {}^1/_4 \ r^w r^w$

(red)   (red)   (silver)   (white)

H. The chance of an offspring having a particular genotype is independent of previous offspring.

Genetics knows no history. Each gamete usually arises independently of all other gametes and thus has the same probability of occurring. Each time you flip a coin, you have a $^1/_2$ chance of flipping a head, regardless of how many heads you have previously flipped.

EXAMPLE: A normal couple had three children, all of whom died of Tay-Sachs disease, a recessive genetic disorder. What is the chance that their next child will have Tay-Sachs?

To produce a child with Tay-Sachs, each parent must be heterozygous; thus the cross is:

$$Tt \times Tt$$

We know that each gamete has a $^1/_4$ chance of being tt. Therefore, there is a $^1/_4$ chance that their next child will be affected.

Summary

1. Situations involving only one gene can yield ratios of: $^3/_4 : ^1/_4$; $^1/_2 : ^1/_2$; $^1/_4 : ^1/_2 : ^1/_4$; $^2/_3 : ^1/_3$.
   Look at the ratios in the progeny; if one of the ratios is seen, there is probably one gene.
2. Try diagramming the cross using one gene. If you can get the observed ratio, there is probably only one gene.
3. If the observed ratios do not agree with expected single gene ratios, you must consider more than one gene (see chapter 2).

Practice Problems

1. Blue diaper syndrome is a rare inborn error of human metabolism. Certain amino acids are not absorbed in the small intestine and are excreted, causing a blue color in the feces.
   a. If two normal individuals have an affected child, what is the mode of inheritance of the disease?
   b. What is the chance that the second child will be affected?

2. In peas, a cross between a yellow plant and a green plant yields 61 yellow and 57 green plants. Diagram the cross.

3. In *Drosophila,* a cross between two flies with short bristles yields 43 short and 25 normal.
   a. What is the mode of inheritance of the short bristles?
   b. What ratio do you expect if you cross a short-bristled fly with a normal fly?
   c. What ratio do you expect if you cross two normal flies?

4. If two black dogs are crossed, seven black and two brown pups result.
   a. Which allele is dominant?
   b. Which allele is recessive?
   c. What is the genotype of the parents?

5. In the human ABO blood system, the alleles A and B are dominant over O. What possible phenotypic ratios do you expect from a mating between an A individual and a B individual?

6. Two short-tailed cats are mated. In the progeny, two have no tails, six have short tails, and three have long tails. Explain these results by diagramming the cross.

7. In *Drosophila*, two red-eyed flies mate and yield 140 red and 48 bright orange. Diagram the cross and determine which allele is dominant.

8. Based on the following crosses in sheep, determine the genotype of each individual.

Cross	Progeny
white-1 × white-2	6 white : 1 black
white-1 × white-3	5 white
white-1 × black-1	3 white : 3 black

9. In *Drosophila*, red eyes (se^+) is dominant over sepia eyes (se). Two heterozygous red-eyed flies are crossed, and one of the red-eyed progeny is backcrossed to a red-eyed parent. What is the chance of the backcross offspring being sepia?

10. In horses, repeated matings between two palaminos yielded seven chestnut, 11 palamino, and six cremello.
    a. Explain these results by providing genotypes of the different phenotypes.
    b. What cross would produce the largest percentage of palaminos?

11. In rabbits, four alleles of a single gene are involved in coat color. These alleles exhibit a dominance hierarchy:

$$C \text{ (gray)} > c^{ch} \text{ (chinchilla)} > c^h \text{ (Himalayan)} > c \text{ (albino)}$$

In addition, $c^{ch}c^h$ and $c^{ch}c$ are light gray.

A gray rabbit is crossed with the following rabbits to yield the following progeny:

Cross	Progeny
gray × chinchilla	6 gray, 5 light gray
gray × light gray	8 gray, 3 light gray, 4 Himalayan
gray × albino	9 gray, 8 Himalayan

Determine the genotypes of the four individuals.

12. Human hair color comes in five shades, exclusive of red: blond, light brown, medium brown, dark brown, and black. Crosses between different colors yield the following results:

blond × blond $\longrightarrow$ all blond

black × black $\longrightarrow$ all black

blond × medium brown $\longrightarrow$ all light brown **or**
    $^1/_2$ blond : $^1/_2$ medium brown

medium brown × medium brown : all medium brown **or**
    $^1/_2$ dark brown : $^1/_2$ light brown **or**
    $^1/_2$ medium brown : $^1/_4$ black : $^1/_4$ blond

   a. Determine the genotypes of all five hair colors.
   b. What would you expect if you crossed light brown with dark brown?
   c. What would you expect if you crossed light brown with black?

13. A soybean plant with dark green leaves is pollinated by a plant with light green leaves and yields equal numbers of dark green and light green plants. If two of the light green progeny are crossed, 29 dark green and 57 light green plants result. Explain these results.

14. Can two individuals with type A blood produce any children with:
   a. type O blood?
   b. type B blood?

15. The flowers of the imaginary plant *Chromus baffleus* may be red, pink, or white. From the following crosses, deduce the genotypes of the parents.

Cross	Progeny
red-1 × pink	$^2/_3$ red, $^1/_3$ pink
red-1 × white	$^1/_2$ red, $^1/_2$ pink
red-2 × pink	$^1/_2$ red, $^1/_4$ pink, $^1/_4$ white
red-3 × pink	all red
red-3 × white	all red

Chapter 2

Two or More Genes

A. The presence of four phenotypes in the progeny suggests at least two genes.

Recall that if only one gene is involved, only three genotypes (and hence three phenotypes) can result: *AA, Aa, aa.*

EXAMPLE: In peas, a cross between two yellow, smooth plants produces progeny that are yellow, smooth; yellow, wrinkled; green, smooth; and green, wrinkled. What is the nature of the inheritance?

We see four phenotypes and hypothesize that two genes are involved. Even in the absence of numbers for the progeny, we can deduce that yellow and smooth must be dominant to green and wrinkled, respectively. If either were recessive, the individual would have been homozygous for the trait; therefore, only one class should have appeared.

B. The genotypes of the parents can be determined by examining single gene ratios in the progeny.

Unlinked genes will assort independently. By looking for single gene ratios — 1:0, 3:1, 1:1, and 1:2:1—you should be able to determine the genotypes of the parents.

EXAMPLE: Consider the following crosses and determine the genotypes of the parents in each cross.

Cross	Progeny			
	yellow, smooth	yellow, wrinkled	green, smooth	green, wrinkled
yellow, smooth × yellow, smooth	45	15	16	5
yellow, wrinkled × yellow, wrinkled	0	42	0	15
green, smooth × yellow, wrinkled	31	30	36	33

In the first cross, look at the yellow-to-green ratio, 60:21—almost exactly 3:1. Therefore yellow is dominant and both parents must be heterozygous. Now look at smooth-to-wrinkled ratio, 61:20. Again, we see a 3:1 ratio, indicating smooth is dominant and heterozygous in each parent. Thus, the cross is probably *Yy Ss × Yy Ss.*

In the second cross, there are no smooth progeny. Therefore, the wrinkled progeny are either homozygous; or wrinkled is dominant; and at least one parent is homozygous. In the absence of cross one, we can't determine the mode of inheritance of wrinkled. We can, however, conclude that yellow is dominant (we got a 3:1 ratio) and that it is heterozygous in each parent (See chapter 1 if this statement is not clear). Based on cross 1, we can conclude that this cross is *Yy ss* × *Yy ss*.

In the third cross, in the absence of the other crosses, we see 61 yellow to 69 green and 67 smooth to 63 wrinkled. Both of these ratios are 1:1, and we can conclude that these ratios result from matings between a heterozygote and homozygous recessive. With only this cross, we can't determine dominance; if we use all three crosses, we see that the cross is *yy Ss* × *Yy ss*.

C. A 9:3:3:1 ratio in the progeny suggests two unlinked genes, a mating between two double heterozygotes, and a strict dominant-recessive relationship.

EXAMPLE: True-breeding flies that have long wings and dark bodies are mated to true-breeding flies with short wings and tan bodies. All the F_1 have long wings and tan bodies. The F_1 are allowed to mate and produce:

> 88 tan, long
> 32 dark, long
> 28 tan, short
> 12 short, dark

What is the mode of inheritance?

From the F_1 we can see that long and tan must be dominant, and the F_2 result confirms this assumption. We see a 3:1 ratio for both tan : dark and long : short. The total number of flies is 160. An ideal 9:3:3:1 would be 90:30:30:10. Our results are very close to this. Therefore we conclude that tan and long are dominant and the F_1 were heterozygous.

D. A 3:3:1:1 ratio in the progeny suggests two genes, one heterozygous in each parent and one heterozygous in one parent and homozygous recessive in the other.

EXAMPLE: A brown-eyed, long-winged fly is mated to a red-eyed, long-winged fly. The progeny are:

> 51 long, red
> 53 long, brown
> 18 short, red
> 16 short, brown

What are the genotypes of the parents?

Examine each trait separately. There are 104 long : 34 short and 69 red : 69 brown. Length appears in a 3:1 ratio; therefore, long is dominant and each parent is heterozygous. Eye color appears in a 1:1 ratio. We can't determine which allele is dominant; all we can conclude is that one parent is homozygous recessive and that one parent is heterozygous. If *L* = long, *l* = short, *R* = red, and *r* = brown, one possible way to indicate the cross is:

Ll rr × *Ll Rr*

E. The presence of four equally frequent classes (1:1:1:1) in the progeny suggests two genes and a double heterozygote × double recessive.

EXAMPLE: A tall, green plant is mated with a short, yellow plant and produces:

> 30 tall, green
> 28 tall, yellow
> 32 short, green
> 27 short, yellow

What are the genotypes of the parents?

We see four phenotypes, so we must have two genes. We can't determine which allele is dominant, but we do see 58 tall : 59 short and 62 green : 55 yellow. Each of these is a 1:1 ratio. If T = tall, t = short, Y = yellow, and y = green, the cross might be:

$$Tt\ yy \times tt\ Yy$$

Note that a 1:1:1:1 ratio requires that one parent be heterozygous and the other homozygous for each gene. Crosses of the form $Aa\ Bb \times aa\ bb$ and $Aa\ bb \times aa\ Bb$ both yield a 1:1:1:1 ratio.

F. With dominance, the presence of more than four phenotypes in the progeny suggests more than two genes.

Two genes, with pure dominance, yield only four phenotypes: dom-dom; dom-rec; rec-dom; rec-rec. Also, the number of phenotypes is 2^n, where n = number of genes. Thus for three genes, we expect eight phenotypes.

Note: The above statement holds only in the case of strict dominance. If we have two genes, and each exhibits incomplete dominance, we expect 3^2 phenotypes from the following genotypes: *AABB, AABb, AAbb, AaBB, AaBb, Aabb, aaBB, aaBb, aabb* (see chapter 1 for discussion of incomplete dominance).

EXAMPLE: In peas, tall is dominant to short, yellow is dominant to green, and smooth is dominant to wrinkled. If a plant heterozygous for all three genes is selfed (self-pollinated), what phenotypes do you expect?

List the possible genotypes:

T-Y-S-	tall, yellow, smooth
T-Y-ss	tall, yellow, wrinkled
T-yy S-	tall, green, smooth
T-yy ss	tall, green, wrinkled
tt Y-S-	short, yellow, smooth
tt Y-ss	short, yellow, wrinkled
tt yy S-	short, green, smooth
tt yy ss	short, green, wrinkled

G. The chance of getting a specific genotype or phenotype is the product of individual probabilities.

EXAMPLE: Consider the cross in part **F**, *Tt Yy Ss* × *Tt Yy Ss*. What is the chance of getting a plant that is:

1. tall, yellow, smooth?
2. short, green, wrinkled?
3. tall, green, smooth?

You could set up a Punnett square and count the boxes, but unfortunately this is an 8 × 8 matrix and yields 64 squares to count—very tedious. Set up the cross:

$$Tt\ Yy\ Ss\ \times\ Tt\ Yy\ Ss$$

and look at one gene at a time.

In the first question, the chance of getting each dominant trait is ¾. Therefore the chance of all three together is ¾ × ¾ × ¾ = ²⁷⁄₆₄.

In the second question, the chance of getting each recessive trait is ¼. Therefore the chance of all three is ¼ × ¼ × ¼ = ¹⁄₆₄.

In the third question, the chance of short is ¼, chance of green is ¼, and chance of smooth is ¾. Therefore the total chance is ¼ × ¼ × ¾ = ³⁄₆₄.

H. The product rule can be used to calculate ratios for any cross, even if lethals are involved.

EXAMPLE: In flies, curly wings *(Cy)* is dominant to straight *(cy)*, but homozygous curly flies do not hatch. Ebony body *(e)* is recessive to tan body *(E)*. What phenotypic ratio among the progeny do you expect if you cross two flies that are heterozygous for the two genes?

Write the cross:

$$Cycy;\ Ee\ \times\ Cycy;\ Ee$$

and use the product rule.

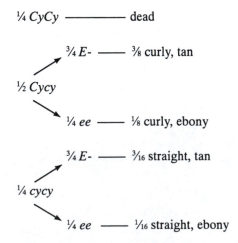

¼ *CyCy* ———— dead

½ *Cycy*
  ¾ *E-* —— ⅜ curly, tan
  ¼ *ee* —— ⅛ curly, ebony

¼ *cycy*
  ¾ *E-* —— ³⁄₁₆ straight, tan
  ¼ *ee* —— ¹⁄₁₆ straight, ebony

But we need to note that this total does not equal one. We can only count the flies that live. Convert all the fractions to sixteenths (¹²⁄₁₆ alive and ⁴⁄₁₆ dead), and then determine the ratio to yield:

6 curly, tan
2 curly, ebony
3 straight, tan
1 straight, ebony

I. If a cross between two individuals with the same mutant phenotype yields all wild-type progeny, two different genes are responsible for the mutant phenotype.

EXAMPLE: In *Drosophila*, a cross between two true-breeding individuals with bright orange eyes produces progeny all with red, wild-type eyes. Explain this observation.

Assume that the mutant phenotype is dominant and only one gene is involved. The cross could then be *AA × AA, AA × Aa,* or *Aa × Aa*. The first two possibilities predict all mutant progeny; the last possibility predicts both wild and mutant progeny. Neither prediction agrees with the results; therefore, the genes are not dominant.

If the mutant trait were recessive, the cross would then be *aa × aa,* and all the progeny should be mutant. Since neither possibility fits the results, we must have more than one gene involved.

If either of two recessive genes alone can produce the mutant phenotype, the cross could be:

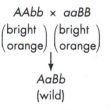

$$AAbb \times aaBB$$
$$\binom{\text{bright}}{\text{orange}} \binom{\text{bright}}{\text{orange}}$$
$$\downarrow$$
$$AaBb$$
$$(\text{wild})$$

J. Interaction between two genes produces a variant of a 9:3:3:1 ratio in the progeny.

EXAMPLE: Consider a cross between individuals heterozygous for two genes, *A* and *B*. What phenotypic ratios are possible in the progeny?

List the expected phenotypes:

9/16 *A- B-*
3/16 *A- bb*
3/16 *aa B-*
1/16 *aa bb*

If either mutant gene alone produces a mutant phenotype, the genotypes *A- bb, aa B-,* and *aa bb* are mutant, and a 9:7 ratio results. Note that this ratio resembles a 1:1 from a testcross, but that in a testcross, the parents have different phenotypes.

If one mutant gene masks the effect of the other gene, all individuals homozygous recessive for one gene, *aa bb* and *aa B-,* will be mutant, and a 9:4:3 ratio results. This ratio resembles a 1:2:1 ratio for incomplete dominance. But in incomplete dominance, individuals used for the cross may have an intermediate phenotype.

All other modifications of a 9:3:3:1 ratio can and do exist: 9:6:1, 15:1, 12:3:1, and 13:3. If you have two or three phenotypes in the progeny, test the results first for one gene. If the predictions from a single gene are inconsistent with the results, try two genes with gene interaction. If you have two genes, each exhibiting incomplete dominance, the following ratio is expected: 1*AA BB* : 2*AA Bb* : 1*AA bb* : 2*Aa BB* : 4*Aa Bb* : 2*A ab* : 1*aa BB* : 2*aa Bb* : 1*aa bb*.

K. Always work from the simple to the complex.

EXAMPLE: In corn, the genotype *A- C- R-* is colored. Individuals homozygous recessive for at least one gene are colorless. Consider the following crosses involving colored plants all with the same genotype. Based on the results, deduce the genotype of the colored plant.

Parents	Progeny
colored × *aa cc RR*	½ colored; ½ colorless
colored × *aa CC rr*	¼ colored; ¾ colorless
colored × *AA cc rr*	½ colored; ½ colorless

First list all possible genotypes for colored plant:

AA CC RR
AA CC Rr
AA Cc RR
AA Cc Rr
Aa CC RR
Aa CC Rr
Aa Cc RR
Aa Cc Rr

The first genotype can be eliminated because all progeny should be colored, regardless of the tester strain.

AA CC Rr can be eliminated since all progeny in the first cross would have been colored.

AA Cc RR can be eliminated since all progeny in the second cross would have been colored.

Aa CC RR can be eliminated since all progeny in the third cross would have been colored.

We are now left with:

AA Cc Rr
Aa CC Rr
Aa Cc RR
Aa Cc Rr

Try *AA Cc Rr* × *aa cc RR* and use the product rule.

1*A-* × ½ *C-* × 1*R-* = ½ *A-C-R-* colored. This could be the genotype, so try this strain in the second cross.

AA Cc Rr × *aa CC rr*

$1 A- \times 1 C- \times \frac{1}{2} R- = \frac{1}{2}$ colored. Not the observed results, therefore not *AA Cc Rr*.

Now try *Aa CC Rr* × *aa cc RR:*

$\frac{1}{2} A- \times 1 C- \times 1 R- = \frac{1}{2}$ *A-C-R-* colored; this fits the results.

Try *Aa Cc RR* × *aa cc RR:*

$\frac{1}{2} A- \times \frac{1}{2} C- \times 1 R- = \frac{1}{4}$ colored; this does not fit the results; the genotype is not *Aa Cc RR*.

Now try *Aa Cc Rr* × *aa cc RR:*

$\frac{1}{2} A- \times \frac{1}{2} C- \times 1 R- = \frac{1}{4}$ colored; not seen; not *Aa Cc Rr*.

Therefore the genotype must be *Aa CC Rr*. Confirm this with the other two crosses.

Aa CC Rr × aa CC rr:

$\frac{1}{2} A- \times 1 C- \times \frac{1}{2} R- = \frac{1}{4}$ colored; fits.

Aa CC Rr × AA cc rr:

$1 A- \times 1 C- \times \frac{1}{2} R- = \frac{1}{2}$ colored; fits.

Summary

1. Four phenotypes usually indicates two genes.
2. More than four phenotypes and dominance suggests more than two genes.
3. Two genes, each heterozygous, gives a 9:3:3:1 ratio, or a modified form of this ratio.
4. The product rule can be applied to predict phenotypic ratios.

Practice Problems

1. Consider the following crosses in *Drosophila*. Based on the results, deduce which alleles are dominant and the genotypes of the parents.

Parents	Progeny			
	brown, long	brown, vestigial	red, long	red, vestigial
brown, long × brown, long	78	24	0	0
red, long × red, vestigial	30	27	98	95
red, vestigial × red, long	0	0	80	87
red, long × red, long	45	16	139	51
red, vestigial × brown, long	48	42	46	45

2. Consider the following cross in nematodes:

dumpy, coordinated × long, uncoordinated

↓

47 dumpy, coordinated; 45 long, coordinated
53 dumpy, uncoordinated; 56 long, uncoordinated

What are the genotypes of the parents?

3. A cross between a purple and a white martian produces all purple progeny. If the F_1 are selfed, the following colors appear in the F_2 progeny: purple, white, red, blue, and brown. What can you conclude about the mode of inheritance?

4. Two deaf individuals mate and produce three offspring who all can hear. If two of the offspring are mated, what fraction of the progeny will be deaf?

5. In *Drosophila,* a dominant gene hairless *(H)* produces flies with no bristles; hairless is lethal in the homozygous condition. An independent dominant gene, Suppressor of hairless *(S)* suppresses the hairless phenotype when present. *S* has no phenotype in combination with *hh.* If two flies that are both heterozygous for both genes are mated, what phenotypic ratio is expected?

6. In humans, blue eyes, albinism, PKU, and galactosemia are controlled by four independent recessive genes. A normal man who is heterozygous for all four genes marries a blue-eyed, galactosemic woman who is heterozygous for albinism and PKU. What is the chance of their first offspring:
   a. showing all dominant traits?
   b. being blue-eyed, PKU, and galactosemic?
   c. being a blue-eyed albino who is also galactosemic?

7. Consider the following two crosses:

	Cross A	Cross B
P	*AaBb* × *AaBb*	*AaBb* × *AaBb*
F_1	15 dom : 1 rec	9:4:3

   a. What phenotypic ratio in the F_1 do you expect if the P from *A* is testcrossed?
   b. What phenotypic ratio in the F_1 do you expect if the P from *B* is testcrossed?

8. For the following cross,

Aa Bb cc Dd × *Aa bb CC Dd*

   what is the chance of obtaining an individual who:
   a. shows all dominant traits?
   b. shows all recessive traits?
   c. is *phenotypically* like the second parent?
   d. is *genotypically* like the second parent?
   e. is heterozygous for all genes?

9. Many matings between a dark, short-haired dog and a dark, long-haired dog yield the following progeny:

    36 dark, short
    39 dark, long
    11 albino, short
    13 albino, long

Explain these results.

10. Polydactyly (a rare trait resulting in extra digits on hands or toes) and tongue curling are independent dominant traits in humans. A man has polydactyly and his wife does not. Both can curl their tongues, but neither of their fathers could. What is the chance of this couple having a child who is:
    a. normal with a straight tongue?
    b. polydactylic with a curling tongue?

11. Consider the following martian crosses involving a true-breeding purple and three different true-breeding white lines.

	Cross 1:	Cross 2:	Cross 3:
P	purple × white-1;	purple × white-2;	purple × white-3
F_1	18 purple	17 purple	18 purple
F_2	95 purple	79 purple	54 purple
	31 white	36 white	32 white
		28 red	19 red
			17 blue
			6 brown

    a. What is the genotype of each white parent?
    b. What phenotypic ratio do you expect if the F_1 of cross 2 is crossed with white-2?
    c. What phenotypic ratio do you expect if the F_1 from cross 3 is mated with white-3?
       (Courtesy of P. J. Bruns)

12. A cross between two pure-breeding white-flowered plants produces all white F_1s. If the F_1s are selfed, 104 white and 24 red-flowered plants are produced.
    a. Explain these results by providing the genotypes of all individuals.
    b. What result do you expect if the F_1s are backcrossed to each of the parents?

13. In mice, any individual who is cc is albino. Two other allele pairs, A/a and B/b, in the presence of C, produce gray, black, cinnamon, and chocolate. Four pure-breeding, genotypically-distinct albino lines are crossed to true-breeding grays (AA BB CC). The F_1s are all gray. The F_1s from each cross are allowed to mate among themselves to produce the following F_2s:

Albino line	Gray	Black	Cinnamon	Chocolate	Albino
1	44	0	16	0	20
2	31	0	0	0	9
3	48	15	0	0	21
4	145	43	46	15	82

What is the genotype of each albino line?

14. A true-breeding scarlet-eyed fly is crossed to a true-breeding brown-eyed fly to yield all red F_1s. The F_1s are crossed to yield 92 red, 28 brown, 31 scarlet, and 9 white. Explain these results.

15. A dog breeder made the following repeated crosses and obtained the following results:

Cross	Progeny
golden female × golden male	6 golden : 1 black : 1 brown
golden female × black male	4 golden : 3 black : 1 brown

Explain these results by providing the genotypes of the three dogs.

16. Suppose that the following genotypes produce the following phenotypes:

A- B- : red
A- bb : prune
aa B- : scarlet
aa bb : white

A third recessive genotype *cc* kills all individuals who are homozygous for prune, but has no effect on other genotypes. Similarly, *C-* has no phenotype. If two individuals that are heterozygous for each gene mate, what phenotypic ratio do you expect in the progeny?

Chapter **3**

Meiosis

A. Meiosis separates maternal and paternal chromosomes and yields cells with one-half the original number of chromosomes.

EXAMPLE: *Drosophila* have eight chromosomes (four pairs) in each somatic cell. How many chromosomes are there in the gametes?

One-half of eight is four. But the four chromosomes must represent each of the four different types of chromosomes in the parents. The following diagrams summarize this concept. Paternal chromosomes are stippled and maternal chromosomes are unmarked. Each chromosome, in this case, carries one gene indicated by the letters A through D.

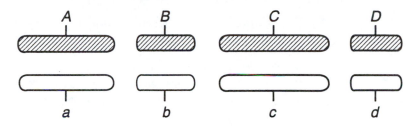

After meiosis the gametes must get one copy of each chromosome; for example:

Note that many different combinations of paternal and maternal chromosomes are possible (see concept 3-B). Meiosis explains the segregation of alleles.

B. The number of different chromosomal combinations in gametes is 2^n, where n = number of different chromosomes (haploid number).

EXAMPLE: An organism has three different chromosomes called A A′, B B′, C C′, where chromosomes from the father are marked with a prime and chromosomes from the mother are unmarked. How many different kinds of gametes can this organism produce?

Each gamete must get one A, one B, and one C chromosome. Since $n = 3$, we expect eight different gametes. They can be deduced empirically:

> A B C
> A B C′
> A B′C
> A B′C′
> A′B C
> A′B C′
> A′B′C
> A′B′C′

C. Organisms with an odd number of sets of chromosomes (e.g., triploids) are usually sterile.

EXAMPLE: An organism has three copies of one chromosome, A, A´, and A´´. What kinds of gametes will it produce?

If all three chromosomes attach to the same spindle, one cell will get two chromosomes and one cell will get only one chromosome. Thus, possible gametes can be: AA´ and A´´; AA´´ and A´; or A and A´A´´. Fertilization of a gamete with one chromosome (monosomic) by a similar monosomic gamete produces a zygote with two chromosomes (disomic, or in this case, diploid). Fertilization of a disomic by a disomic produces a zygote with four copies of the chromosome, and fertilization of a disomic by a monosomic produces a trisomic. As the number of chromosomes increases, the chance of producing a zygote with the correct number of chromosomes becomes increasingly small. Most zygotes will have an unbalanced set with either extra chromosomes or a subnormal number of chromosomes. Such zygotes usually will not survive, or at best will be severely abnormal. In many cases, the gamete with fewer than normal chromosomes will not survive either.

D. A diploid cell just prior to meiosis has twice as many DNA molecules as it has chromosomes.

Chromosomal duplication is a necessary prerequisite for meiosis. Immediately prior to meiosis, each chromosome has two chromatids (DNA molecules) attached to one centromere. A truly haploid cell will have one DNA molecule per chromosome.

EXAMPLE: *Drosophila* have four pairs of chromosomes. How many DNA molecules are present in a cell at the end of meiosis I? At the end of meiosis II?

It helps to draw the chromosomes at different stages. A diploid cell will have eight chromosomes. Remember, one DNA per chromatid.

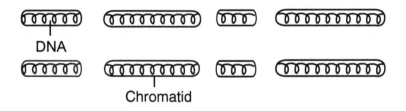

During S phase, the chromatids (DNA) double.

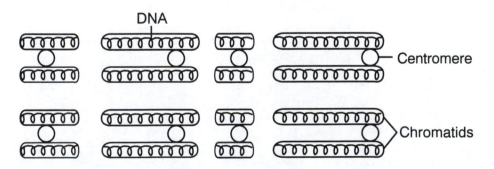

Therefore, just prior to meiosis, there are 16 DNA molecules (8 chromosomes × 2 DNA strands per chromosome). After meiosis I each cell looks like this:

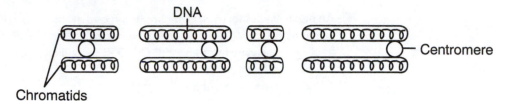

Chromatids

There are four duplicated chromosomes. Therefore, after meiosis I there are 4 chromosomes × 2 DNAs/chromosome = 8 DNA.

Meiosis II separates the chromatids:

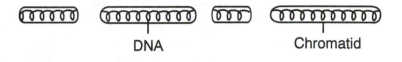

DNA   Chromatid

Therefore, the resultant haploid cell has four single chromosomes and hence, four DNA strands.

Summary

1. Meiosis cuts the number of chromosomes in half.
2. The number of different gametes is 2^n, where n = number of different chromosomes.

Practice Problems

1. Dogs have 78 chromosomes.
   a. How many pairs of chromosomes do they have?
   b. How many chromosomes are in the gametes?
2. An organism has a diploid number of 12. Designate these chromosomes as: *Aa, Bb, Cc, Dd, Ee, Ff.*
   a. How many different chromosomal combinations can appear in the gametes?
   b. What is the chance of a gamete getting all capital chromosomes?
3. How many different chromosome combinations can be produced by the human female?
4. Humans have 23 pairs of chromosomes. If the amount of DNA in the egg is represented as *c*, what is the amount of DNA in:
   a. a cell after meiosis I?
   b. a diploid cell that has just divided mitotically?
   c. a cell just prior to the start of meiosis?
5. A plant has four pairs of chromosomes designated as: *AA, BB, CC* and *DD*. If this plant is self-fertilized, what chromosome complement(s) would be found in the roots of the offspring?

   a. *A B C D*   d. *AA BB CC*   g. *AA BB DD*
   b. *B C D*   e. *CC DD*   h. *AAAA BBBB CCCC*
   c. *A B C*   f. *AA BB CC DD*

6. An organism has three pairs of chromosomes. Let the chromosomes from the male parent be P, Q, and R, and those from the female parent be P´, Q´, and R´. What fraction of the gametes from a PP´ QQ´ RR´ individual will be:
   a. all of paternal origin?
   b. all of maternal origin?
   c. two of maternal origin and one of paternal origin?

7. Wheat has $2n = 42$ and corn has $2n = 20$. Explain why a corn-wheat hybrid is usually sterile.

8. In rye, the haploid number is seven. How many chromosomes would you expect to find in:
   a. the tube nucleus?
   b. a leaf cell?
   c. the endosperm?

9. How many sperm will be formed from:
   a. 60 primary spermatocytes?
   b. 60 secondary spermatocytes?
   c. 60 spermatids?

10. In humans, how many eggs will come from:
   a. 60 primary oocytes?
   b. 60 secondary oocytes?

11. An organism has eight pairs of chromosomes. In the absence of crossing over, how many different chromosomal combinations are possible for the gametes?

Chapter 4

X-Linkage

A. In most animals, sex is determined by the type of sperm that fertilizes the egg.

For many animals, males are XY and females are XX. Meiosis in females produces gametes that all contain an X chromosome. In males, even though the X and Y chromosomes are different, they pair during meiosis and attach to the same spindle. The result is that half of the sperm get an X chromosome and half get a Y chromosome. If an X-bearing sperm fertilizes an egg, the zygote is XX, and hence female. If a Y-bearing sperm fertilizes the egg, an XY zygote results, and this organism is usually male.

B. Males give their X chromosome to all their daughters and their Y chromosome to all their sons.

Since females are XX, they must get an X chromosome from each parent. Since males are XY, they must get the X from the mother and the Y from the father. Implicit in the above statement is that Y-linked traits are passed only from father to son.

Note: In some animals, such as many birds, the male is the homogametic sex (i.e., it has two identical sex chromosomes). To avoid confusion, these are indicated as ZZ. The female is the heterogametic sex, and therefore has two different sex chromosomes, indicated as ZW. In such cases, recessive traits show up in the female F_1 rather than the male F_1.

EXAMPLE: A male canary showing a recessive sex-linked gene is mated to a female canary with the dominant allele. In the progeny, which sex, if any, will show the dominant trait and which, if any, will show the recessive trait?

Remember, in birds, the female is ZW and the male is ZZ. Let Z^A = the dominant allele and Z^a = the recessive allele. Since the male shows the recessive trait, he must be Z^aZ^a; the female is Z^AW. The cross is then:

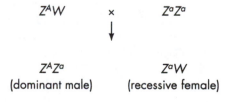

$$Z^AW \quad \times \quad Z^aZ^a$$

$$\downarrow$$

$$Z^AZ^a \qquad\qquad Z^aW$$

(dominant male)   (recessive female)

C. A phenotypic difference between male and female progeny should suggest sex-linkage (either X-linkage or Y-linkage).

EXAMPLE: A female fly with white eyes is crossed to a male with red eyes. All the female progeny are red and all the male progeny are white. What is the mode of inheritance?

We see differences between the sexes, suggesting some type of sex linkage. If eye color is determined by a gene on the Y chromosome, all sons should be red. This is not seen; therefore, eye color must be carried on the X chromosome. Since females have two X chromosomes, and because all females are red, red must be dominant to white. Since all the males have the same phenotype, the female parent must be homozygous.

If we let X^+ = red and X^w = white, the cross is then:

$$X^w X^w \quad \times \quad X^+ Y$$
$$\text{(white)} \quad \downarrow \quad \text{(red)}$$

$$X^+ X^w \qquad X^w Y$$
$$\text{(red)} \qquad \text{(white)}$$

D. A female heterozygous for an X-linked trait should produce two different types of male progeny in equal frequencies.

EXAMPLE: A male and female fly, each with red eyes, are mated. All female progeny have red eyes, half of the males have red eyes, and half of the males have white eyes. What is the mode of inheritance, and what are the genotypes of the parents?

We deduce that we are dealing with X-linkage because of the differences between sexes. Since all females are red, red must be dominant, and the male must be $X^R Y$. Since half the males are white, the female must be heterozygous. We can diagram the cross as follows. Let X^R = red, and X^r = white.

$$X^R X^r \quad \times \quad X^R Y$$
$$\text{(red)} \quad \downarrow \quad \text{(red)}$$

$$X^R X^r \quad X^R X^R \qquad X^R Y \quad X^r Y$$
$$\text{(red)} \quad \text{(red)} \qquad \text{(red)} \quad \text{(white)}$$

E. If all the female progeny from an affected male show a trait, the trait is probably inherited as an X-linked dominant.

EXAMPLE: In a hypothetical organism, a black-haired male is mated to a brown-haired female. All the female progeny are black-haired; all of the males are brown-haired. What is the mode of inheritance and what are the genotypes of the parents?

X-linkage must be involved because we see a difference between males and females. Since the male has only one X chromosome and since all the females are black, black must be dominant. If black is dominant, the female must be homozygous, since we see only one phenotype in the males. Let X^B = black and X^b = brown. We can then diagram the cross as:

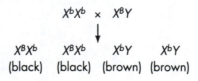

$$X^b X^b \quad \times \quad X^B Y$$
$$\downarrow$$

$$X^B X^b \quad X^B X^b \qquad X^b Y \quad X^b Y$$
$$\text{(black)} \quad \text{(black)} \quad \text{(brown)} \quad \text{(brown)}$$

F. A 3:3:1:1 ratio in the progeny may suggest two genes, one autosomal and one X-linked.

EXAMPLE: Based on the following *Drosophila* crosses, explain the genetic basis for each trait and determine the genotypes of all individuals.

P: white-eyed, dark-bodied female × red-eyed, tan-bodied male

F_1: females: all red, tan
 males: all white, tan

F_2: 27 red, tan
 24 white, tan
 9 red, dark
 7 white, dark,
(No differences between males and females in F_2.)

We see four phenotypes, so we must have at least two genes involved (see chapter 2). We see no difference in body color between sexes, so we can conclude that body color is autosomal.

Note that if body color were X-linked, males should have had dark bodies. Since all F_1 have tan bodies, tan must be dominant to dark.

We see a difference in eye color between the sexes in the F_1, suggesting that eye color is X-linked. Since the F_1 females have red eyes, red must be dominant and, hence, the original white-eyed female must be homozygous for the recessive allele.

In the F_2, the tan to dark ratio is 51:16, very close to the 3:1 ratio expected for one autosomal gene (see chapter 1). The ratio of red to white is 36:31, very close to the expected 1:1 ratio for an X-linked trait.

Let + = tan body, dk = dark body, X^R = red, X^r = white. We can diagram the cross between the F_1:

$$+/dk \; X^R X^r \quad \times \quad +/dk \; X^r Y$$

This cross yields:

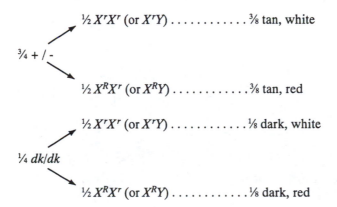

$\frac{3}{4} +/-$

$\frac{1}{2} X^r X^r$ (or $X^r Y$) . . . . $\frac{3}{8}$ tan, white

$\frac{1}{2} X^R X^r$ (or $X^R Y$) . . . . $\frac{3}{8}$ tan, red

$\frac{1}{4} dk/dk$

$\frac{1}{2} X^r X^r$ (or $X^r Y$) . . . . $\frac{1}{8}$ dark, white

$\frac{1}{2} X^R X^r$ (or $X^R Y$) . . . . $\frac{1}{8}$ dark, red

Note that if the cross had been set up the other way:

red, tan female × white, dark male

we would have seen different results. All the F_1 of both sexes would have been red and tan. In the F_2, we would have seen:

Females	Males
¾ red, tan	⅜ red, tan
¼ red, dark	⅜ white, tan
	⅛ red, dark
	⅛ white, dark

You should work through this reciprocal cross to convince yourself of this ratio. Notice that in this case, we have no indication of X-linkage until the F_2. Any phenotypic difference between males and females usually indicates that the trait is X-linked.

G. An X-linked lethal will reduce the number of male progeny.

EXAMPLE: A female fly with notched wings is mated to a male with normal wings. The progeny are:

> 35 notched females
> 39 normal females
> 33 normal males

What is the mode of inheritance of the notched phenotype?

Notice that we see only normal males but both normal and notched females. This difference again suggests X-linkage. Since we see two types of females, notch must be dominant. If it were recessive, all females should have been normal. All females get a normal X chromosome from the male. The fact that we see some normal females suggests that the original female is heterozygous. The 2:1 female-to-male ratio suggests that some of the males die. These must be the males that receive the notched X chromosome. Notched must be dominant, but lethal in the homozygous or hemizygous state.

If X^N = notch and X^n = normal, we can thus diagram the cross:

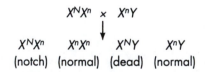

The $X^N Y$ flies must die.

H. In mammals, the appearance of different phenotypes in different cells, or in different regions of the same animal, may suggest that the trait is X-linked.

In mammals, the Lyon hypothesis proposes that all X chromosomes in excess of one are inactivated. This hypothesis means that in any given cell of a female, only one of the two X chromosomes is active. If the activation is random, we expect to see areas where one chromosome is active and areas in which the homolog is active. Implicit in this statement is that we usually expect to see *mosaics* only in heterozygous females. The rare mosaic male must be XXY (see chapters 6 and 7).

EXAMPLE: An orange male cat is crossed to a black female cat. All the male progeny are black and all the females show areas of black and areas of orange. Explain these results.

The different phenotypes between sexes suggests X-linkage. The female must be homozygous for black, since all the males are black. The patches of black and orange in the females can be explained by random inactivation of one of the two X chromosomes in females. Let X^B = black and X^O = orange. The cross can be diagrammed as:

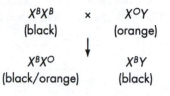

If black is dominant, all F_1 females should be black, and this result is not seen.

Summary

1. We detect sex-linkage by seeing a phenotypic difference between males and females.
2. Heterozygous females produce males in a 1:1 phenotypic ratio.
3. Males give their X chromosome to their daughters and their Y chromosome to their sons.
4. One autosomal and one X-linked gene may give a 3:3:1:1 ratio.
5. X-linked lethals reduce the number of males.

Practice Problems

1. Hemophilia is an X-linked recessive disorder. A normal woman whose father was hemophilic marries a normal man. They have a hemophilic son. The man claims his wife has been unfaithful. If you were a judge, how would you rule and why?
2. In hippies, formerly thought to be extinct, the X-linked trait frizzled hair is dominant to straight hair. Devise a breeding program so that the sex of the offspring can be determined merely by looking at the hair texture.
3. A female fly that has red eyes and short wings is crossed to a male with brown eyes and long wings. All the F_1 have red eyes and long wings. The F_1 mate to produce:

Females	Males
75 long, red	39 long, red
23 short, red	37 long, brown
	14 short, red
	10 short, brown

What are the modes of inheritance of the genes and what are the genotypes of the parents?
4. A female *Drosophila* with short bristles is mated to a male with long bristles. The progeny are 42 long-bristled females, 40 short-bristled females, and 43 long-bristled males.
   a. What is the mode of inheritance of the short bristles?
   b. What phenotypic ratio do you expect if you cross two long-bristled flies?

5. A black and orange female cat is crossed to an orange male, and the progeny are:

    females: 3 orange, 3 orange and black
    males: 2 black, 2 orange

    Explain these results.

6. A yellow male canary is crossed to a green female. All the males are green and all the females are yellow. Explain these results.

7. Consider the following crosses in canaries:

Parents	Progeny
yellow male × yellow female	all yellow
yellow female × green male	all green
green female × yellow male	all yellow females
	all green males

    Explain these results by determining which allele is dominant and how color is inherited.

8. Consider the following cross involving yellow and gray true-breeding *Drosophila*:

Cross	F_1	F_2
gray female × yellow male	all gray males	95 gray females
	all gray females	40 yellow males
		45 gray males

    Based on the above results, what do you expect in the F_1 and F_2 if you cross a true-breeding yellow female and a true-breeding gray male?

9. You discover a man with scaly skin. He marries a woman with normal skin. They have four daughters, all with scaly skin, and three sons with normal skin. The sons all marry women with normal skin, and all their children have normal skin. One of the daughters marries a man with normal skin, and they have two scaly daughters, one normal daughter, one scaly son, and one normal son.
    a. How is scaly skin inherited?
    b. Based on your answer to (a), what is the chance that the next child of the above couple will have scaly skin?

10. In *Drosophila*, yellow body is an X-linked recessive trait, and vestigial wings is an autosomal recessive trait. A homozygous yellow female is crossed with a homozygous vestigial male.
    a. What phenotypic ratio do you expect in the F_1?
    b. What phenotypic ratio do you expect in the F_2?
    c. Suppose the initial cross were reversed: vestigial female × yellow male. What phenotypic ratio do you expect in the F_2?

11. In *Drosophila*, an orange-eyed female is mated with an orange-eyed male to yield all red F_1s of both sexes. The F_1s are allowed to interbreed and produce:

Females	Males
245 red	119 red
75 orange	201 orange

Explain these results.

12. In *Drosophila*, notched wing is an X-linked dominant trait that is hemizygous lethal; vermillion eyes is an X-linked recessive trait; and ebony body is an autosomal recessive trait. A notched, red-eyed, tan-bodied female is mated with a normal-winged, red-eyed, ebony male to yield ⅓ notched, red, tan females; ⅓ normal, red, tan females; and ⅓ normal, vermillion, tan males.
  a. What is the genotype of each parent?
  b. What phenotypic ratio do you expect if you cross the F_1 males to normal-winged F_1 females? to notched-winged F_1 females?

13. A white-eyed male fly is crossed with a brown-eyed female. All the F_1s have wild-type red eyes. The F_1s are selfed to produce:

Females	Males
red-eyed 450	red-eyed 230
brown-eyed 145	white-eyed 305
	brown-eyed 68

Provide an explanation for these results.

14. The enzyme 6-PGD is composed of two subunits. A single X-linked gene in both *Drosophila* and man is responsible for this protein. Two alleles, *6-PGD^A* and *6-PGD^B* are known in both species. In the heterozygous female, how many different forms do you expect to find in:
  a. *Drosophila*?
  b. in adult humans?

Chapter 5

Linkage

A. Departure from expected ratios should suggest linkage.

EXAMPLE: Consider the cross *Aa Bb* × *aa bb* to yield:

> 42 *A-B-*
> 39 *aa bb*
> 10 *A-bb*
> 9 *aaB-*

What information can be deduced from this cross?

This is a testcross and we expect a 1:1:1:1 ratio. Notice that the single gene ratios are as expected: 52 *A-* : 48*aa* and 51*B-* : 49*bb*. The expected ratio is for two *independent* genes. Genes *A* and *B* do not seem to be behaving independently; 80 percent of the time the two alleles stay together. This can only happen if genes *A* and *B* are on the same chromosome. If the two genes were completely linked, we would see 50 percent *A-B* and 50 percent *aabb*. We calculate the recombination frequency (RF) as:

$$\text{recombinants/total} \times 100 = 19/100 \times 100 = 19\%.$$

EXAMPLE: *AaBb* × *AaBb* yields:

66 *A-B* : 16 *aabb* : 9*A-bb* : 9*aaB-*

Note that the expected 9:3:3:1 ratio is not seen. The double recessive individual shows up much more frequently than expected. We conclude that linkage is occurring, but it is difficult to calculate RF because some of the recombinant classes are masked.

B. The most frequent classes will be the parental, non-recombinant classes.

Recombination is a rare event. Most of the time parental chromosomes will not exchange.

EXAMPLE: Consider the cross in the first example in concept A. How are the alleles arranged in the heterozygote?

We have deduced that genes *A* and *B* are linked. The heterozygote could be either *AB/ab* or *Ab/aB*. Since the most frequent classes are *A-B-* and *aabb*, these must represent non-recombinant chromosomes. Therefore, the alleles are in *cis* or *coupling*, represented as *AB/ab*.

C. Linkage does not change the expected numbers of phenotypes; only the frequencies are changed.

EXAMPLE: Consider again the first example in concept A. We still saw four phenotypes. The frequency with which the minority phenotypes appear depends upon the distance between the two linked genes. Similarly, for three linked genes, we still expect eight phenotypes.

D. In a testcross, two equally frequent majority classes and two equally frequent minority classes suggest linkage.

EXAMPLE: Refer again to the first example in concept A. We deduced linkage initially because of altered ratios. Closer examination of the results indicates that *A-B-* and *aabb* are equally frequent; *A-bb* and *aaB-* are also equal, but are in a minority. If the genes were not linked, we would expect a 1:1:1:1 ratio.

E. Reciprocal classes usually appear equally frequently.

Recombination results in the exchange of parts of homologous chromosomes. The event that produces one recombinant class also produces the other class. If we draw homologous chromosomes and indicate an exchange as follows:

the resultant chromosomes will be

A___b and a___B

Similarly, if there is no recombination, one gamete gets *A___B* and the other gets *a___b*.

F. In crosses involving three genes that are each heterozygous, double crossover classes will usually be the least frequent.

EXAMPLE: Consider the cross

$$\frac{A\_b\_C}{a\_B\_c} \times \frac{a\_b\_c}{a\_b\_c}$$

What phenotypic classes should be least frequent?

Recombination is a rare event. The chance of two rare events occurring within the same meiosis is approximately the product of the individual chances; hence this would be a very rare event.

Draw the chromosomes and double exchange:

The gametes that result from this double exchange will be:

A___B___C and a___b___c

Thus the two phenotypic classes *ABC* and *abc* will be the least frequent. In some cases with three linked genes, you will see only six or seven phenotypic classes. If you see only six phenotypes, and the two missing classes are reciprocal, the missing classes are then the double crossover (DCO) classes.

EXAMPLE: *AbC/aBc* × *abc/abc* yields:

AbC	40
aBc	38
ABc	6
abC	5
aBC	5
Abc	3
ABC	3

What is the observed frequency of DCO?

These results require a little thought, since we see almost equal numbers in five different classes. Classes *abC* and *aBC*, although equal, are not reciprocal classes. One class, *abc*, is missing. We can therefore group the progeny in the following way:

AbC and aBc	78
ABc and abC	11
aBC and Abc	8
ABC and abc	3

The last classes are the least frequent and hence the double crossover classes. Thus the frequency of double crossovers is 3/100 × 100 = 3%. Notice that reciprocal classes are grouped together.

G. A double crossover changes the association of the middle gene.

EXAMPLE: A triple heterozygote for three linked genes *A, B,* and *C* is crossed to a homozygous recessive individual and produces:

Abc and aBC	125
ABC and abc	35
ABc and abC	30
AbC and aBc	10

What is the gene arrangement in the heterozygote and what is the gene order?

The most frequent classes are *Abc* and *aBC*, and must represent non-recombinant chromosomes. The parent is therefore *Abc/aBC*. Note that this notation does not convey gene order at the moment; it merely indicates that the dominant *A* allele is associated with the recessive *b* and *c* alleles.

We use the least frequent classes, the DCO, to determine gene order. These classes are *AbC* and *aBc*. Compare these classes with the non-recombinant, parental classes. *Ab* and *aB* are still together, just as they were in the parents. The *C* allele has been transposed so that *A* and *C* are now associated. *C* must be in the middle. Confirm this conclusion by drawing the double crossover:

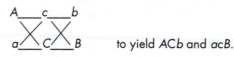

to yield *ACb* and *acB*.

H. To establish a map, first determine gene order, then calculate distances between middle gene and end genes.

EXAMPLE: Consider the three linked genes in corn: $+/b$; $+/lg$; $+/v$. A testcross between a triple heterozygote and a homozygous recessive yields the following progeny:

$$165 + v\ lg$$
$$125\ b + +$$
$$64\ b + lg$$
$$56 + v +$$
$$37 + + lg$$
$$33\ b\ v +$$
$$11 + + +$$
$$9\ b\ v\ lg$$

TOTAL 500

Determine the genetic composition of the heterozygote; determine gene order and map distances; and calculate the coefficient of coincidence.

1. Determine the non-recombinants as the most frequent. In this case they are $+v\ lg$ and $b + +$. Therefore the heterozygote is $+ v\ lg/b + +$.

2. Determine the order by comparing the DCO classes to the parental classes. In this cross, $+ + +$ and $b\ v\ lg$ are the least frequent. Since v and lg are together in the parent, only b has been exchanged. Therefore b is in the middle, and we can redraw the heterozygote as:

$$\frac{v\_\_+\_\_l}{+\_\_b\_\_+}$$

3. Calculate RF between v and b by using all crosses where b and v (and $+$ and $+$) now appear together. $(37 + 33 + 11 + 9)/500 = 90/500 \times 100 = 18$ map units.

4. Calculate RF between b and lg by using all classes in which b and lg appear together. $(64 + 56 + 11 + 9)/500 = 140/500 \times 100 = 28$ map units.
   We can thus draw the following map:

$$v\_\_\_18\_\_\_b_____28\_\_\_\_lg$$

5. Calculate the coefficient of coincidence (CC).

$$CC = \text{observed DCO/expected DCO}$$

Expected DCO $= (0.28)(0.18) = 0.05$

$0.05 \times 500 = 25$. We observe 20 DCO. Therefore CC $= 20/25 = 0.8$

I. To predict frequencies when distances are known, first calculate the expected frequency of double crossovers, then subtract this number from the given distances.

EXAMPLE: Consider three genes linked in the following manner:

$$A\_\_30\_\_\_\_B\_\_\_20\_\_\_C$$

If a triple heterozygote AbC/aBc is crossed to abc/abc, what phenotypic ratios do you expect? Assume that the frequency of DCOs is the product of single exchanges (no interference).

Since this is a testcross, the frequency of gametes will equal the frequency of phenotypes.

1. Calculate frequency of DCO. These classes will be *ABC* and *abc*.

$$DCO = (0.3)(0.2) = 0.06$$

Since recombination is reciprocal, ½ (0.06) will represent each class: 0.03 *ABC* and 0.03 *abc*.

2. Calculate single exchange between *A* and *B*. Recall that RF between *A* and *B* was 0.3, which equals the sum of singles plus doubles divided by the total. Therefore,

0.30 – 0.06 = 0.24. The classes *ABc* and *abC* will each be 0.12.

3. Calculate the frequency of single exchanges between *B* and *C*.

0.20 – 0.06 = 0.14. The frequency of *Abc* and *aBC* will each be 0.07.

4. Calculate non-recombinants by subtracting all recombinants from one.

1.00 – 0.44 = 0.56. The classes *AbC* and *aBc* will each be 0.28.

In some cases, the occurrence of one exchange inhibits (or enhances) a second exchange nearby. This phenomenon is called interference (I), and is calculated as I = 1– CC. For the above problem, assume that the interference is 0.2, and calculate the expected frequencies. To do so the expected frequencies of DCO must first be modified.

Since I = 1 – CC, CC = 0.8.

$$CC = observed\ DCO/expected\ DCO$$
$$0.8 = observed/0.06$$
$$observed = 0.8 \times 0.06 = 0.048$$

Therefore the DCO classes will be 0.048, and singles between *A* and *B* will be:

$$0.300 – 0.048 = 0.252$$

Singles between *B* and *C* will be:

$$0.200 – 0.048 = 0.152$$

Non-recombinants = 0.548

J. The presence of four equally frequent majority classes and four equally frequent minority classes suggests that two genes are linked and one gene is not.

EXAMPLE: A triple heterozygous female fly *+/sc; +/ec; +/vg* is crossed to a triple homozygous recessive male. All mutant traits are recessive. The progeny are:

sc ec vg	233
+ + +	239
sc ec +	241
+ + vg	231
sc + vg	12
+ ec +	14
sc + +	14
+ ec vg	16
TOTAL	1000

Explain these results by drawing a suitable map.

We expect a 1:1:1:1:1:1:1:1 ratio if all three genes are unlinked. Since this ratio is not seen, some of the genes must be linked. The four majority classes must represent non-recombinants combined with independent assortment. If all three genes were linked, we would see only two majority classes.

To determine which two genes are linked, examine two genes at a time. Look at *ec* and *vg* within the majority classes.

$$
\begin{array}{lll}
ec & vg & 233 \\
+ & + & 239 \\
ec & + & 241 \\
+ & vg & 231 \\
\end{array}
$$

This ratio is an expected 1:1:1:1. Therefore, *ec* and *vg* are not linked.

Now try *sc* and *ec*.

$$
\begin{array}{lll}
sc & ec & 233 \\
+ & + & 239 \\
sc & ec & 241 \\
+ & + & 231 \\
\end{array}
$$

Among the majority classes we see only two combinations. Therefore *sc* and *ec* are linked. The four minority classes represent recombination between *sc* and *ec*.

$$RF = (12 + 14 + 14 + 16)/1000 = 56/1000 \times 100 = 5.6 \text{ map units.}$$

K. In *Drosophila*, a 5:1:1:1 ratio suggests linkage between two genes more than 50 map units apart.

EXAMPLE: Two *Drosophila*, heterozygous in coupling for the linked recessive traits brown eyes and black bodies are crossed to yield:

    52 tan, red
     9 tan, brown
    10 black, red
     9 black, brown

Explain these numbers by drawing a genetic map.

Let + = red, *br* = brown, + = tan, *b* = black. The cross is then:

$$br\ b/+\ +\ \times\ br\ b/+\ +$$

We conclude that the two genes are linked since we don't see a 9:3:3:1 ratio. Note that this cross is not a testcross, so it is difficult to estimate RF. Remember there is no crossing over in *Drosophila* males. Thus the male produces only two kinds of gametes: +__+ and *br*__*b*. The female produces four kinds of gametes: +__+, +__*b*, *br*__+, and *br*__*b*. If these two genes are more than 50 map units apart, they behave as independent genes, and four gametes have an equal chance of appearing.

	++	br b
++	++/++	++/brb
brb	++/brb	brb/brb
+b	++/+b	+b/brb
br+	++/br+	br+/brb

This yields:

5 ++/-   tan, red
1 br+/brb tan, brown
1 +b/brb   black, red
1 br b/brb black, brown

Note: If the two genes are linked in repulsion, a 2 wild : 1 brown : 1 black ratio results. Work through the cross to convince yourself that this indeed is the observed ratio.

L. Map distances are approximately additive, thus allowing many genes to be ordered.

EXAMPLE: Given the following gene-to-gene distances, determine a map that includes all genes.

O–R	3	R–A	13	R–G	5
M–R	7	G–A	8	O–G	8
M–G	12	G–N	10	O–N	18

Start with genes with large distances; they must be near the ends. Then place other distances to generate overlapping maps.

O_____18_____N

M_____12_____G__10__N

Now look at R–G = 5. If R is to the right of G, M–R must be about 17. This is not seen, so R is to the left of G.

M____7__R_5__G_____10___N

If O is to the right of N, O–R should be very large, but this is not seen. Therefore, O is to the left of N. Since O–R=3 and O–G=8, O must be between M and R.

M__O_3__R___5__G____10_____N

Since M–R = 7, M–O must be 4. A can be on either side of G. If A is to the right of G, R–A = 13. The complete map is thus:

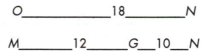

M__4_O_3_R__5__G___8__A_2_N

Summary

1. Linkage is usually detected as variations from expected ratios.
2. Recombinants/total × 100 gives recombination frequency.
3. Double crossovers are usually the least frequent classes.
4. Always group reciprocal classes together.
5. Map distances are usually additive.
6. A 5:1:1:1 ratio in *Drosophila* suggests two genes in coupling that are linked by more than 50 map units.
7. In crosses involving three or more genes, an unlinked gene will result in four equally frequent majority classes and four or more minority classes.

Practice Problems

1. In rabbits, unspotted *(W)* is dominant to spotted *(w)* and short *(S)* is dominant to long *(s)*. Females heterozygous for both genes are mated to homozygous recessive males to yield:

   75 spotted, long
   66 unspotted, short
   10 unspotted, long
   7 spotted, short

   a. Are the two genes linked?
   b. What is the chromosome composition of the female?
   c. If the genes are linked, estimate the map distance.

2. In a fictitious organism, the autosomal alleles tall *(T)* and rough skin *(R)* are dominant to short *(t)* and smooth *(r)* respectively. Heterozygous tall, rough females were crossed to short, smooth males and yielded the following progeny:

tall, rough	105
tall, smooth	263
short, rough	273
short, smooth	110

   a. Are the two genes linked? Why or why not?
   b. In the heterozygous females, how were the tall and rough alleles arranged? Explain.
   c. Calculate the percentage recombination between the two genes.

3. Derive a map based on the following recombination frequencies.

c–b : 9	d–e : 10	a–b : 3	b–d : 12
a–f : 7	c–f : 13	f–d : 8	a–e : 25

4. Consider the following cross involving three linked genes *DeF/dEf* × *def/def*. Determine the gene order.

DeF	76
def	30
dEf	82
DEF	24
Def	15
DEf	1
dEF	18
deF	4
TOTAL	250

5. In a fictitious organism, a dumpy, white, straight female is mated to a slim, black, bent male to yield all slim, white, straight F_1. The F_1 female was mated with a dumpy, black, bent male and yielded the following progeny:

slim, white, straight	169
slim, black, straight	19
slim, black, bent	301
dumpy, white, bent	21
slim, white, bent	8
dumpy, black, bent	172
dumpy, black, straight	6
dumpy, white, straight	304
TOTAL	1000

   a. Construct a genetic map giving gene order and all distances.
   b. Calculate the coefficient of coincidence.

6. In *Drosophila*, kidney bean eye *(k)*, cardinal eye *(cd)*, and ebony body *(e)* are three linked recessive alleles. If homozygous kidney, cardinal females are mated to homozygous ebony males, the F_1s are all wild-type. If heterozygous F_1 females are mated with kidney, cardinal, ebony males, the following 1000 progeny result:

kidney, cardinal	440
ebony	443
kidney, ebony	32
cardinal	34
ebony, cardinal	23
kidney	25
kidney, cardinal ebony	1
wild-type	2

   a. Determine the chromosome composition of the F_1 females.
   b. Derive a map of all three genes.

7. True-breeding dumpy-winged, brown-eyed female *Drosophila* are mated to true-breeding wild-type males. The F_1s are all wild-type. The F_1s are selfed to produce:

    110 wild
    17 dumpy
    13 brown
    20 dumpy, brown

Explain these results.

8. In catfish, a trihybrid round, slimy, spiked female was testcrossed with a flat, spineless, smooth male and produced the following offspring:

round, smooth, slimy	145
round, smooth, slimeless	38
round, spiked, slimy	138
round, spiked, slimeless	33
flat, spiked, slimy	40
flat, spiked, slimeless	133
flat, smooth, slimy,	35
flat, smooth, slimeless	148
TOTAL	710

    a. Determine which pair of alleles are linked.

    b. Determine the genotype of the heterozygote, being sure to indicate which alleles are on which chromosomes.

    c. Calculate the map distance between the linked genes.

9. In Teenage Mutant Ninja Turtles, amiable *(A)* is dominant to nasty *(a)*; benign *(B)* is dominant to active *(b)*; crazy *(C)* is dominant to sane *(c)*. A true-breeding amiable, active, sane turtle is mated to a true-breeding nasty, benign, crazy turtle. The F_1s are mated to a nasty, active, sane turtle to produce:

amiable, benign, crazy	192
amiable, benign, sane	208
amiable, active, crazy	780
amiable, active, sane	810
nasty, benign, sane	790
nasty, benign, crazy	820
nasty, active, crazy	195
nasty, active, sane	205
TOTAL	4000

Explain these results and draw a map.

10. Two genes *Q* and *R* are linked by 15 map units. If a heterozygous female in repulsion is testcrossed, what phenotypic frequencies do you expect in the progeny?

11. Consider three recessive genes, *fz, b,* and *stw,* located on the second chromosome of *Drosophila*. The distances between the genes are:

$$fz\_\_\_\_\_15\_\_\_b\_\_\_7\_\_\_stw$$

If + *b stw/fz* + + females are crossed to *fz b stw/fz b stw* males, what will the expected frequencies of phenotypic classes be if the coefficient of coincidence = 0.6?

12. Genes *a* and *b* are linked by 10 map units. Genes *c* and *d* are linked by 5 map units on a chromosome different than the one containing *a* and *b*. An individual homozygous for all dominant alleles is mated to an individual homozygous for all recessive alleles. The F_1s are then testcrossed. Which phenotypic classes will be the least frequent?

Chapter 6

Human Genetics

Many of the concepts in this chapter have already appeared in chapters 1, 2, and 4. You should refer to these chapters before proceeding. Often human pedigrees do not contain enough information to determine unambiguously the mode of inheritance.

A. Individuals showing a dominant trait will usually be heterozygous for the mutant allele.

All mutations are rare events. The chance of an individual having both dominant alleles is the square of the chance of getting one allele. Moreover, often the damage done to cells by two dominant mutant alleles is so severe that the homozygous individual does not survive.

B. If a trait skips a generation, it is probably recessive.

EXAMPLE: In the following pedigree, what is the probable mode of inheritance?

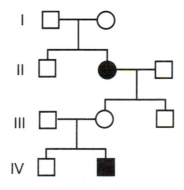

We see that the trait skips generations, so it is probably autosomal recessive. If it were X-linked, the son in generation III would be expected to show the trait, and he doesn't.

C. An X-linked recessive trait may appear in about half of the male progeny from a normal female.

EXAMPLE: From the following pedigree, deduce the mode of inheritance.

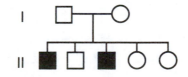

The trait must be recessive since neither parent shows the trait. It is probably X-linked, since ½ of the sons show the trait. If the trait were autosomal recessive, we would expect ¼ of the progeny to show the trait; this is also seen. Thus the trait could be either autosomal or X-linked recessive.

D. A dominant autosomal trait should appear in about half of both sexes of the progeny from an affected individual.

EXAMPLE: Examine the following pedigree and deduce the mode of inheritance.

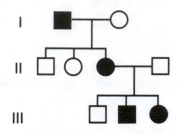

The trait could be autosomal recessive, and the female in I could be heterozygous. An autosomal dominant is also possible, since half of all progeny are affected. The latter possibility is more likely because mutations are rare events. If it were recessive, the chance of a homozygous recessive individual mating with a heterozygote would be very rare.

E. An X-linked dominant trait should appear in all of the daughters of an affected male.

EXAMPLE: What is the likely mode of inheritance of the following trait?

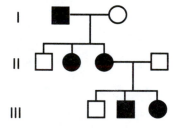

Note that all daughters of the affected male have the trait, so it is probably X-linked dominant. It could also be autosomal recessive *(aa × Aa)* or autosomal dominant *(Aa × aa)*.

F. Y-linked traits will appear only in the sons of affected males.

The male always contributes his Y chromosome to his male progeny; thus any trait that is on the Y will appear only in male progeny.

EXAMPLE: Based on the following pedigrees, what is the probable mode of inheritance?

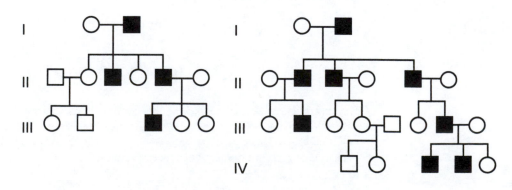

We see that only males have the trait in each generation. An autosomal dominant trait could exhibit this behavior, but it is likely that some of the female progeny would show the trait. The trait is almost certainly carried on the Y chromosome.

G. In pedigrees, assume that normal individuals are homozygous unless contrary evidence is available.

Mutations are rare events, and it is unlikely that a normal individual, in the absence of other information, is heterozygous.

EXAMPLE: What is the chance that the couple in II will have an affected child?

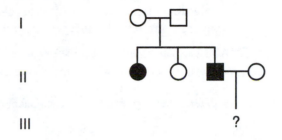

First, try to deduce the mode of inheritance. Since two normal individuals have affected children, the trait must be recessive. It can't be X-linked, for if it were, the male in I would have to have the trait in order for the daughters to have it. Therefore the trait must be autosomal recessive, and II-3 is homozygous. Since the trait is rare, it is unlikely that the wife in II is heterozygous. If we assume she is homozygous, there is no chance of their children having the trait *(aa × AA)*.

H. To calculate the probability of a given genotype, use the product rule.

EXAMPLE: An albino woman has two normal daughters who each marry normal men and have normal children. What is the probability that a first cousin marriage will produce an albino child?

Draw the pedigree and assign genotypes. Assume all men in I and II are homozygous.

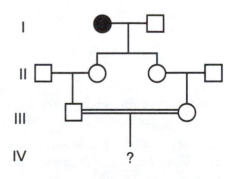

Both daughters must be heterozygous, *Aa*, and the husbands can be assumed to be *AA*. Therefore, each child in III has a probability of ½ of being heterozygous. The probability of both children in III being heterozygous is ½ × ½ = ¼. If two heterozygotes mate, there is a ¼ chance of getting a homozygous recessive individual. Therefore, the chance of an albino in IV is ¼ × ¼ = ¹⁄₁₆.

I. The chance of one or more alternatives is the sum of the probabilities of each event.

EXAMPLE: PKU and albinism are two unlinked autosomal, recessive disorders in humans. If a male and female who are each heterozygous for both traits marry, what is the chance that their first child will be either albino or have PKU?

First, calculate the chance of each trait separately. Let P/p = normal/PKU, and A/a = normal/albino. The cross is $Pp\,Aa \times Pp\,Aa$. Each trait has a 1/4 chance of appearing in a child. For either trait, we add the probabilities: $\frac{1}{4} + \frac{1}{4} = \frac{1}{2}$.

J. For n offspring, the chance of s individuals with one phenotype and t individuals with another phenotype is $\frac{n!}{s!\,t!}\,(p)^s\,(q)^t$ where p and q are the chances of each phenotype occurring.

EXAMPLE: The ability to curl the tongue is a dominant trait in humans. If two heterozygotes have five children, what is the chance that three of them will be curlers?

First determine the probability of each phenotype:

Curler = $\frac{3}{4}$ = p; non-curler = $\frac{1}{4}$ = q

Since three are expected to be curlers, $s = 3$ and $t = 2$. Note that $s + t = n$, and that $p + q = 1$. Substitute these numbers into the formula:

$P = 5!/3!\,2!\,(\frac{3}{4})^3\,(\frac{1}{4})^2 = (5)(4)/2\,(\frac{27}{64})\,(\frac{1}{16}) = \frac{270}{1024} = 0.264$, or about one in four.

For more than two traits, the formula becomes:

$$P = n!/(s!\,t!\,u!...)(p)^s\,(q)^t\,(r)^u...$$

EXAMPLE: If two individuals heterozygous for albinism have five children, what is the probability that they will have two normal sons, two normal daughters, and one albino son? First, assign individual probabilities:

normal son = $(\frac{3}{4})\,(\frac{1}{2}) = \frac{3}{8} = p$
normal daughter = $(\frac{3}{4})\,(\frac{1}{2}) = \frac{3}{8} = q$
albino son = $(\frac{1}{4})\,(\frac{1}{2}) = \frac{1}{8} = r$
albino daughter = $(\frac{1}{4})\,(\frac{1}{2}) = \frac{1}{8} = m$

$$P = 5!/2!\,2!\,1!\,0!\,(\frac{3}{8})^2\,(\frac{3}{8})^2\,(\frac{1}{8})^1\,(\frac{1}{8})^0$$
$$= 30\,(\frac{3}{8})^4\,(\frac{1}{8}) = (30)\,(3)^4/(8)^5 = 2430/32{,}768 = 0.074$$

K. In mouse-human hybrids, a given phenotype will appear in all clones with a particular human chromosome.

EXAMPLE: A given human enzyme is present only in clone B. The human chromosomes present in clones A, B, and C appear below. Determine the probable chromosomal location of the gene for the enzyme.

Clone	1	2	3	4	5	6	7	8
				Human chromosome				
A	+	+	+	+	–	–	–	–
B	+	+	–	–	+	+	–	–
C	+	–	+	–	+	–	+	–

If a gene is located on a chromosome, the chromosome must be present in the positive clones. Chromosomes 1, 2, 5, and 6 are present in *B*. If the gene in question were located on chromosome 1, the enzyme should have been present in all three clones. The only chromosome that is unique to clone *B* is 6. Therefore, the gene is located on chromosome 6.

Summary

1. To analyze pedigrees,
   a. assume a particular mode of inheritance and assign genotypes to affected individuals.
   b. compare predicted progeny and frequency with expected results.
   c. eliminate unlikely or impossible modes of inheritance.
2. In human cell hybrids, look for a chromosome that is unique to the clone(s) that express(es) the given enzyme.

Practice Problems

1. PKU is an inborn error of metabolism of the amino acid phenylalanine. The following pedigree is of an affected family.

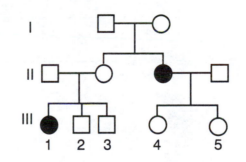

   a. What is the mode of inheritance of PKU?
   b. Which persons are known to be heterozygous for PKU?
   c. What is the probability that III-2 is heterozygous?
   d. If III-3 and III-4 marry, what is the probability that their first child will have PKU?

2. Below is a pedigree for the trait *lingus lanulatis*. What mode(s) of inheritance is (are) not possible for this trait?

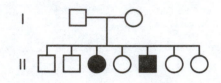

3. For each of the following pedigrees, determine possible modes of inheritance.

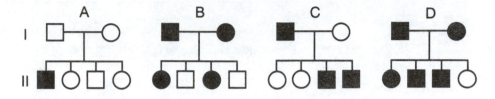

4. You have selected three mouse-human hybrid clones and analyzed them for the presence of human chromosomes. You then analyze each clone for the presence or absence of particular human enzymes (+ = presence of human chromosome or enzyme activity). Based on the results below, indicate the probable chromosomal location for each enzyme.

	Human chromosome						
Clone	2	6	7	10	12	13	22
X	−	+	−	+	+	−	+
Y	+	+	−	+	−	+	−
Z	−	+	+	−	−	+	+

	Enzyme				
Clone	A	B	C	D	E
X	+	−	−	+	+
Y	+	+	+	−	+
Z	+	−	+	−	−

5. Draw a pedigree that would strongly support the following modes of inheritance:
   a. autosomal recessive
   b. X-linked dominant

6. Consider the following pedigree.

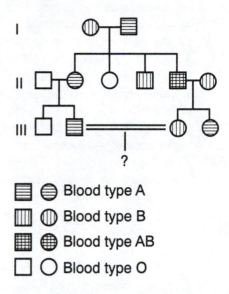

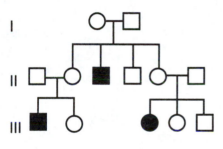

■ ⊖ Blood type A

▥ ⬭ Blood type B

▦ ⊕ Blood type AB

□ ○ Blood type O

What is the chance that the indicated first cousin marriage will produce a child with type O blood?

7. For each of the following pedigrees, determine which mode(s) of inheritance is (are) **impossible.**

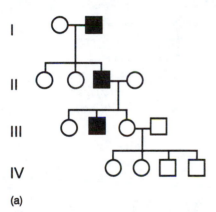

(a)

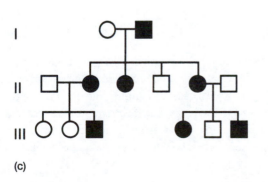

(b)

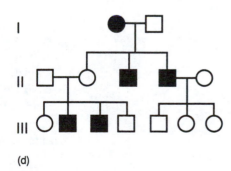

(c)

(d)

8. A man's father died of Huntington's disease, an autosomal dominant trait. Symptoms of the disease do not appear until midlife. There is no history of the disease in the wife's family.
   a. What is the chance that the man will develop the disease?
   b. What is the chance that this couple will have an affected child?

9. In humans, the absence of molars is inherited as an autosomal dominant trait. If two heterozygotes have five children, what is the probability that:
   a. all will have no molars?
   b. three will have no molars and two will have molars?
   c. the first two will have no molars and the last three will have molars?

10. Cystic fibrosis is inherited as a recessive trait. If two normal but heterozygous individuals marry, what is the chance that:
    a. one of three children will be affected?
    b. of four children, the order will be: normal boy, affected girl, affected boy, normal girl?

11. A normal man (1) whose grandfather had albinism, marries a normal woman (2) whose mother was albino. What is the probability that the second child will be normal?

12. The ability to taste phenylthiocarbamide (PTC) is a dominant trait in humans. If a heterozygous taster marries a non-taster,
    a. what is the probability that of their four children, two will be tasters?
    b. what is the probability that of their six children, three will be tasters?

13. In humans, the absence of molars is an autosomal dominant trait, and albinism and Tay-Sachs disease are autosomal recessives. If a man with molars and heterozygous for both albinism and Tay-Sachs marries a woman heterozygous for all three genes, what is the chance of their first child:
    a. having molars, Tay-Sachs, and albinism?
    b. lacking molars or having Tay-Sachs disease?

14. Three mouse-human cell lines were scored for the presence (+) or absence(-) of human chromosomes; the results appear below.

Cell line	Human chromosome							
	1	3	5	7	9	11	13	17
A	+	+	+	+	−	−	−	−
B	+	+	−	−	+	+	−	−
C	+	−	+	−	+	−	+	−

   a. If a particular gene is located on chromosome 11, what clone(s) should be positive for the enzyme?
   b. What clone(s) should be positive if the gene is on chromosome 5?

15. The human disorder *incontinentia pigmenti* is a rare syndrome in which melanin is not retained by melanocytes, causing swirling pigment lines on the skin. A woman with the disorder marries a normal man. She gives birth to three normal daughters, two affected daughters, and two normal sons. In addition, she had three spontaneous abortions of deformed male fetuses. Propose an explanation to account for all these results.

Chapter 7

Chromosomal Changes

A. The lack of two or more expected phenotypes suggests an inversion heterozygote involving linked genes.

Most of the gametes that result from a single crossover within an inversion are inviable because the chromosomal complement is incomplete.

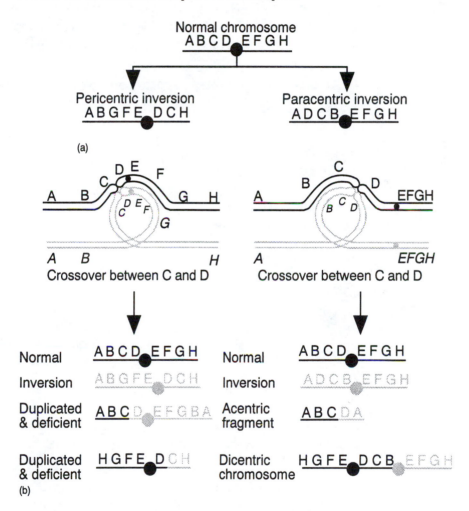

Since all the possible gametes are not produced, certain phenotypic classes will be absent.

EXAMPLE: A heterozygous plant *ABCDE/abcde* is crossed to an *abcde/abcde* plant. The following progeny appear.

> *ABCDE*
> *abcde*
> *Abcde*
> *aBCDE*
> *ABCDe*
> *abcdE*

What is unusual about the results and how can you explain them?

We have five heterozygous genes, so we expect to see 32 phenotypes (see chapter 2), but we only see six phenotypes. We see no exchanges between genes *B*, *C*, and *D*. These three genes could be so tightly linked that no recombination occurs between them. This is unlikely, however. Genes *B*, *C*, and *D* could be within an inversion that is heterozygous in the heterozygous parent. The recombination that does occur within this inversion results in inviable zygotes.

B. If a recessive phenotype appears unexpectedly, consider a deletion.

A deletion of a region on one of the two homologs results in only one copy of a given gene, a situation similar to X-linked genes.

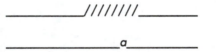

EXAMPLE: A homozygous ebony female fly is crossed to a homozygous wild male that has been X-rayed. Among the progeny is a single ebony fly. Explain this result.

The cross can be diagrammed as:

$$ee \quad \times \quad e^+e^+$$
$$\downarrow$$
$$\text{all } e^+e$$
$$\text{(all wild)}$$

If the male chromosome carries a deletion of the ebony region, an F_1 could look like this:

$$\underline{\qquad\qquad e \qquad\qquad}$$
$$\underline{\qquad /////// \qquad}$$

There is no wild-type allele to mask the ebony allele, so the phenotype is ebony. We could confirm a deletion by crossing the F_1 ebony fly with a wild F_1.

$$\underline{\qquad e \qquad} \qquad \underline{\qquad e \qquad}$$
$$\underline{\quad ///// \quad} \quad \times \quad \underline{\qquad + \qquad}$$
$$1\ e/e : 1\ e/ : 1\ +/e : 1\ +/$$
$$\text{(1 ebony) (1 wild)}$$

The expected result is identical to that expected from a testcross.

C. Deletions are usually lethal in a homozygous condition.

EXAMPLE: Refer again to the example in concept 7-B. Suppose we recovered both a male and female ebony fly from the above cross. What can be said about the relative number of progeny if the two ebony F_1 are crossed?

Diagram the cross:

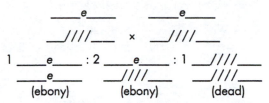

Since ¼ of the progeny are missing part of each chromosome, they will probably not survive. The number of progeny will be only ¾ of what is expected, and all of them will be ebony.

D. Deletions can be used to localize genes to specific regions.

If a gene in question lies within a particular deletion, the amount of enzyme will usually be less (often about 50 percent less) than normal.

EXAMPLE: You are trying to locate a gene in *Drosophila*, and you already know that the gene is located on the second chromosome. You have five strains with deletions for different regions of the second chromosome.

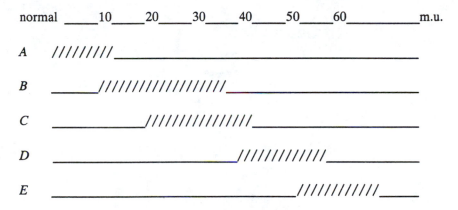

You cross each strain with wild-type flies and measure the amount of enzyme in each F_1. The results appear below. In what region is the gene located?

Strain crossed	Enzyme percentage
A	100
B	48
C	49
D	97
E	101

We see about half the enzyme activity in crosses with strains *B* and *C*. Therefore, the gene must be located in the region that is common to both strains, approximately the region located 25-35 m.u. from the left end.

E. A reduction in the number of expected progeny may suggest a reciprocal translocation.

With reciprocal translocations, only some of the possible chromosomal segregation patterns will yield gametes or zygotes with a full chromosomal complement.

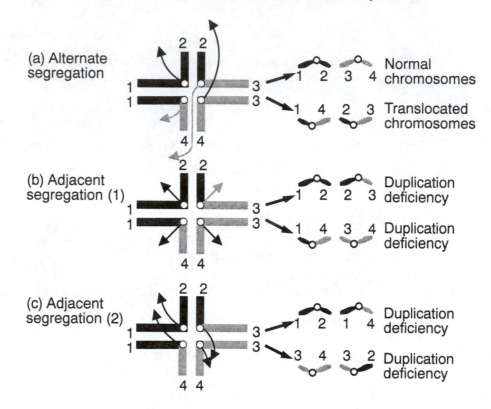

EXAMPLE: Consider the following crosses in corn; then provide an explanation for the results.

P:	strain A ×	strain B ×	strain A ×
	strain A	strain B	strain B
F₁:	513	510	515
F₂:	531	514	341

We see that the F₁s from cross $A \times B$ yield fewer progeny than the other crosses. Something unusual must be involved. One explanation is that one of the strains is homozygous for a reciprocal translocation. The translocation, when heterozygous, results in some inviable gametes or progeny.

F. A chromosomal breakpoint can be treated as another mutation, and hence can be mapped.

EXAMPLE: Below is the map position for three X-linked recessive genes in *Drosophila*.

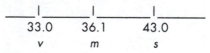

v = vermillion eyes   m = miniature wings   s = sable body

A wild-type male is X-rayed and mated to a vermillion, miniature, sable female. Among the progeny, a single sable (red-eyed, tan-bodied) female is recovered. When this female is mated with a $v\ m\ s$ male, the progeny are:

Females	Males
73 $v\ m\ s$	70 $v\ m\ s$
80 $+ + s$	4 $+ + s$

Explain these results by drawing a genetic map.

The use of X rays alerts us to chromosomal aberrations. The fact that a sable female appears when we expect all wild-type suggests that we have a deletion (see concept 7-B). The deletion must end between s and m. If the deletion included miniature, we should have seen a sable, miniature female. We can draw the chromosomes of the backcross as:

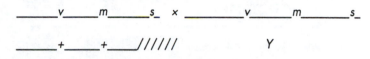

The question is, how far is the deletion from miniature? We must look at the males from the backcross. Note that we only see half as many males compared to females; those males that received the deleted X chromosome must die. The sable males must result from recombination between the end of the deletion and miniature.

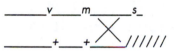

yields the following chromosomes:

__+_____+____s_ and ____v_____m__//////

Therefore, sable males / total males × 100 = R.F.
4/74 × 100 = 5.4 m.u. The chromosomes of the F_1 female can now be redrawn:

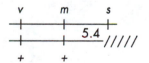

G. Abnormal phenotypes may be the result of aneuploidy.

The genes of a normal organism are finely balanced. Too many chromosomes (such as $2n+1$) or too few chromosomes (such as $2n-1$) usually alters the overall phenotype. Monosomics ($2n-1$) will behave like deletions; recessive alleles will be expressed.

EXAMPLE: The fruit of the normal jimsonweed has a fat, oval shape, with a length-to-width ratio of two. A cross between two normal plants yields an occasional cocklebur fruit that is much thinner than normal (length-to-width ratio between 3 and 4). What might account for the aberrant phenotype?

Fruit shape is almost certainly controlled by more than one gene. The aberrant phenotype suggests some type of aneuploidy. Chromosome analysis will reveal an extra chromosome.

H. If two different species yield fertile hybrids, consider polyploidization.

EXAMPLE: Two old-world species of cotton, A and B, each have 13 pairs of chromosomes. A cross between A and B sometimes yields fertile hybrids. Explain this observation.

Normally interspecific hybrids are sterile because the chromosomes from different species can't pair at meiosis. If each set of chromosomes is duplicated, the duplicated chromosomes will pair, and meiosis will occur normally.

Let A = the haploid set of chromosomes from species A, and B = the haploid set from species B. The typical sterile hybrid has one set A and one set B. If each of these sets doubles, then the hybrid is $AABB$. The A sets and the B sets can now pair, and meiosis can proceed normally. The fertile hybrid probably has $13 \times 2A + 13 \times 2B = 52$ chromosomes, or 26 pairs.

Summary

1. Inversions reduce the number of phenotypic classes.
2. Deletions allow recessive mutations to appear in the F_1.
3. Chromosomal breakpoints can be treated as another gene, and thus mapped.
4. Aneuploids usually have altered phenotypes.
5. Reciprocal translocations are often associated with semi-sterility.

Practice Problems

1. Plant Q has 14 chromosomes and plant R has 20 chromosomes. How many chromosomes will be expected in a fertile QR hybrid?
2. Brown teeth in humans is an X-linked recessive trait. A woman with white teeth whose father had brown teeth marries a man with brown teeth. This couple has a brown-toothed son who is mentally retarded and has poorly formed testes. Account for all these phenotypes and indicate the parent in which nondisjunction probably occurred.
3. Five recessive genes, a, b, c, d, and e, map to the following positions on the second chromosome of *Drosophila*.

```
      a      b        c      d            e
_____|_____|_____|_____|_____|
      10     15       25     30           40
```

A female homozygous for all five genes is crossed to a homozygous wild-type male to yield all wild F_1s. When an F_1 female is crossed to a homozygous recessive male, the following progeny result:

a b c d e	80
+ + + + +	94
a + + + +	6
+ b c d e	4
a b + + +	3
+ + c d e	3
a b c d +	5
+ + + + e	5
TOTAL	200

    a. What is unusual about the results?

    b. What phenomenon will explain these results?

    c. Draw a map of the chromosomes of the F_1 female.

4. Bands one through six of *Drosophila* salivary chromosomes are shown below along with five deletions, A through E. You have six recessive alleles, *p, q, r, s, t,* and *u,* known to be located in this region, but the order of the genes is not known. You produce strains in which each deletion is heterozygous with each allele. In the following table, a letter represents a mutant phenotype and a + represents a wild-type phenotype. Determine which band corresponds to which gene; that is, determine the gene order.

Deletions:

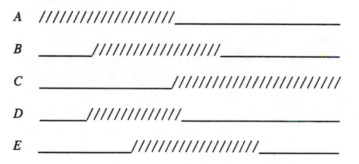

Deletion	Phenotype with respect to:					
	p	*q*	*r*	*s*	*t*	*u*
A	*p*	*q*	*r*	+	+	+
B	*p*	+	*r*	+	+	*u*
C	+	+	+	*s*	*t*	*u*
D	*p*	+	*r*	+	+	+
E	+	+	*r*	+	*t*	*u*

5. A *Sh/Sh* corn plant is crossed to a *sh/sh* plant. The F_1 are semi-sterile and phenotypically *Sh.* The F_1 are crossed to the *sh/sh* plant to yield:

    820 semi-sterile, *Sh*

    800 fertile, *sh*

    195 semi-sterile, *sh*

    185 normal, *Sh*

    a. What genetic phenomenon is involved in this problem?

    b. Draw an appropriate map of the chromosomes of the F_1 plant.

6. A tetraploid with $n = 3$ (*A,B,C*) is crossed with a diploid ($n = 3$) that has the same kinds of chromosomes as the tetraploid (*A,B,C*).

    a. How many chromosomes and how many chromosome sets are there in the hybrid?

    b. Do you expect the hybrid to be sterile or fertile?

7. Yellow body in *Drosophila* is an X-linked recessive trait. A tan-bodied male is irradiated and mated to a yellow female. Among the progeny is a single yellow female.

    a. Why is this result unexpected and how might you explain it?

    b. Predict the progeny if the yellow female, F_1, is mated to a normal, nonirradiated, tan male.

8. Plant species *A* has 2*n* = 22 and species *B* has 2*n* = 12. A fertile hybrid is found. How many chromosomes does it have?

9. A normal-visioned woman whose father was color-blind marries a color-blind male. They have a color-blind daughter with Turner's syndrome (*X0*). In which parent did nondisjunction occur?

10. Explain how an XYY male can be produced.

11. In *Drosophila*, two recessive genes, *a* and *b*, are located at 16.5 and 35.5 on the third chromosome. Wild-type females that are + +/*a b* are mated with *a b*/*a b* males and produce the following progeny:

+ +	500
a b	450
+ *b*	26
a +	24
TOTAL	1000

   a. What is unusual about the results and how can you explain them?
   b. Draw the third chromosomes in the + +/*a b* female.

12. You have four strains of *Drosophila (a–d)* that were isolated in different geographic regions. You compare the banding pattern of the third chromosome and obtain the following results (each number corresponds to a particular band):

a	1 2 6 5 4 3 7 8 9 10
b	1 2 3 4 5 6 7 8 9 10
c	1 2 6 5 8 7 9 4 3 10
d	1 2 6 5 8 7 3 4 9 10

   If *c* is the ancestral strain, in what order did the other strains arise?

13. In *Drosophila*, the recessive gene *yellow* is located near the tip of the X chromosome. A tan male is irradiated and mated with a yellow female. Among the progeny is a single tan male. How can you explain the tan male and how could you test your hypothesis?

14. Down's syndrome in humans results from the presence of extra material from chromosome 21. Usually there are three 21st chromosomes in a Down's patient. Down's can also result from a translocation from part of chromosome 21 to chromosome 15. Assume a normal man is heterozygous for the above translocation.
   a. What kind of gametes will he produce?
   b. What is the chance of this man having a child with Down's syndrome?

15. In *Drosophila*, three X-linked genes, *notch, dwarf,* and *facet*, produce notched wings, small bodies, and rough eyes, respectively. Consider the following crosses:

cross 1:

notch female × *dwarf* male
↓
300 *notch* females
300 *wild* females
300 *wild* males

cross 2:

$$F_1 \text{ notch female } \times \text{ dwarf male}$$

300 *notch* females   300 *dwarf* males
300 *dwarf* females   34 *wild* males
33 *wild* females
33 *dwarf, notch* females

cross 3:

$$\text{dwarf, notch female from cross 2 } \times \text{ facet male}$$

500 *notch, facet* females   500 *dwarf* males
500 *wild* females

cross 4:

$$\text{wild female from cross 3 } \times \text{ wild male}$$

500 *wild* females   220 *dwarf* males
220 *facet* males
30 *dwarf, facet* males
30 *wild* males

a. Are any of the mutations associated with or caused by deletions?

b. Construct the best map for all the data.

Chapter 8

Tetrad Analysis

A. In random spore analysis, map distance between linked genes is calculated as the number of recombinants divided by the total multiplied by 100.

EXAMPLE: In yeast, the following crosses yield progeny as shown. Determine the gene order and distances between the genes.

a^+b^- × a^-b^+		a^+c^- × a^-c^+		b^+c^- × b^-c^+	
a^+b^-	490	a^+c^-	425	b^+c^-	425
a^-b^+	500	a^-c^+	417	b^-c^+	425
a^+b^+	6	a^+c^+	85	b^+c^+	70
a^-b^-	4	a^-c^-	73	b^-c^-	80
	1000		1000		1000

In each cross, the last two classes represent recombinants. Therefore,

$a-b = 10/1000 \times 100 = 1$ m.u.
$a-c = 158/1000 \times 100 = 15.8$ m.u.
$b-c = 150/1000 \times 100 = 15$ m.u.

The gene order becomes _____ *a* _1_ *b* _____ 15_____ *c* __

B. A tetratype results from the exchange between a gene and the centromere.

For two unlinked genes, random alignment at meiosis produces parental ditypes and non-parental ditypes. If the cross is *ab* × ++, then

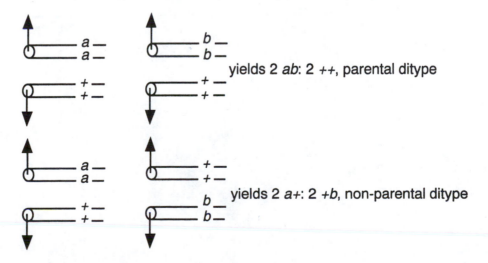

yields 2 *ab*: 2 ++, parental ditype

yields 2 *a+*: 2 +*b*, non-parental ditype

In order to get four different types of spores, there must be an exchange between one gene and its centromere.

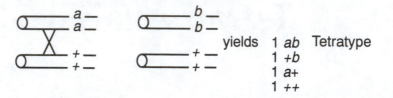

yields 1 *ab* Tetratype
        1 *+b*
        1 *a+*
        1 *++*

EXAMPLE: In a cross of *leu+ his⁻* × *leu⁻ his+*, classify the following asci as parental ditype, non-parental ditype, or tetratype, and indicate which involve recombination between gene and centromere.

I	II	III
leu+ his⁻	*leu+ his+*	*leu+ his⁻*
leu+ his⁻	*leu+ his+*	*leu+ his+*
leu⁻ his+	*leu⁻ his⁻*	*leu⁻ his⁻*
leu⁻ his+	*leu⁻ his⁻*	*leu⁻ his+*

Classes I and II contain only two types of spores, and the spores in I are like the parents. Therefore I is parental ditype (PD) and II is non-parental ditype (NPD). Class III contains four types of spores; hence it is a tetratype (TT), resulting from recombination between a gene and the centromere.

C. If PD >> NPD, the two genes are linked.

Refer to the following figure.

Two genes not linked:

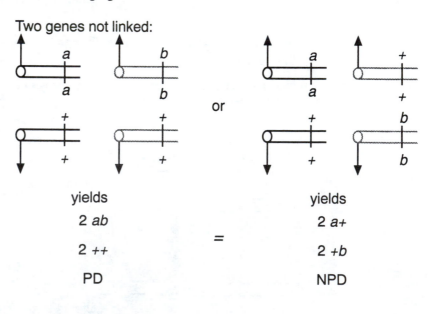

Two genes linked:

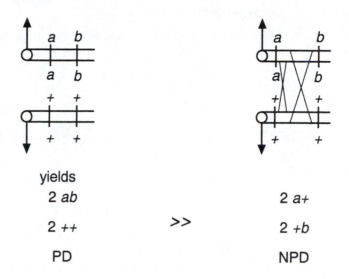

yields

2 ab		2 a+
2 ++	>>	2 +b
PD		NPD

If the two genes are unlinked, PD = NPD due to random alignment at metaphase. If the genes are linked, NPD can only result from a four-strand double crossover, a very rare event.

EXAMPLE: Consider the following crosses in *Chlamydomonas*. For each cross, determine if the two genes are linked.

	PD	NPD	TT	Total
ac+ × +arg	51	49	0	100
ac+ × +pab	88	0	12	100
ac+ × +pf	62	6	32	100
pab+ × +pf	64	4	32	100
pf+ × +thi	29	3	68	100

Compare the number of PD with NPD in each cross. If PD >> NPD, the two genes are linked. Genes *ac, pab, pf,* and *thi* are linked; *arg* is unlinked to these genes.

D. Recombination between two linked genes is calculated by [(½ TT) + NPD]/total × 100.

EXAMPLE: Refer to the crosses in concept C and calculate the gene-to-gene distances.

$ac–pab = [½(12) + 0]/100 × 100 = 6$ m.u.
$ac–pf = [½(32) + 6]/100 × 100 = 22$ m.u.
$pab–pf = [½(32) + 4]/100 × 100 = 20$ m.u.
$pf–thi = [½(68) + 3]/100 × 100 = 37$ m.u.

E. In ordered tetrads, second division segregation is detected by a separation of spore classes.

If the original cross is $a \times +$, first division segregants are:

$$
\begin{array}{ccc}
a & & + \\
a & \text{or} & + \\
+ & & a \\
+ & & a \\
\end{array}
$$

If the two identical alleles are not adjacent, second division segregation occurred:

$$
\begin{array}{cccc}
a & a & + & + \\
+ & + & a & a \\
+ & a & a & + \\
a & + & + & a \\
\end{array}
$$

EXAMPLE: In a *Neurospora* cross of $a+ \times +b$, the following types of asci appear. Classify each type as to the kind of segregation that occurred for each gene.

I	II	III	IV	V	VI
a+	ab	a+	++	a+	ab
+b	a+	a+	ab	+b	++
a+	++	+b	ab	++	ab
+b	+b	+b	++	ab	++

Read down each column and look for those columns in which the pairs of alternate alleles are not adjacent. Classes I, IV, V, and VI show second division segregation for *a*. Classes I, II, IV, V, and VI represent second division segregation for *b*.

F. In ordered tetrads, the gene-to-centromere distance is calculated by (½ second division segregation)/total × 100.

In order to get second division segregation, there must be an exchange between the gene and the centromere.

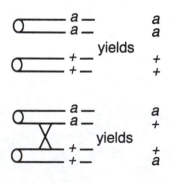

EXAMPLE: In *Neurospora*, three genes, *b*, *c*, and *d*, are crossed in pairwise combinations. Based on the results below, calculate the gene-to-centromere distances.

$$b+ \times +c$$

b+	++	+c
b+	++	++
+c	bc	bc
+c	bc	b+
70	4	26

$$c+ \times +d$$

c+	cd	cd	cd	c+	cd	c+
c+	cd	c+	+d	+d	++	+d
+d	++	++	++	+d	++	++
+d	++	+d	c+	c+	cd	cd
42	2	30	15	5	1	5

Look for second division segregation. We see none for *b*, so *b*-cent = 0 (*b* is linked to the centromere). In both crosses, we find 26 asci with second division segregation for *c*.

Therefore, *c*-cent = ½ (26)/100 × 100 = 13 m.u. For *d*, we see 41 such asci; therefore *d*-cent = ½ (41)/100 × 100 = 20.5 m.u.

Summary

1. Map distances in random spore analysis are calculated as they are in diploids.
2. Detect linkage by observing PD >> NPD.
3. Gene-to-gene distance is calculated by [(½TT) + NPD]/total × 100.
4. Gene-to-centromere distance is calculated by (½ second division segregation)/total × 100.

Practice Problems

1. The following random spores are recovered from a cross of *a*++ × +*bc*. Derive a map for the three genes.

abc	52	a++	102
ab+	34	+b+	8
a+c	6	++c	28
+bc	112	+++	58
TOTAL	400		

2. You have isolated a new fungus and have obtained an *nic⁻* and a *thi⁻* auxotroph. You cross these two strains and collect 500 spores that you plate on minimal medium. Thirty-five of the spores grow. What is the distance between the two genes?
3. Consider the following crosses and ordered tetrads. Draw a map of all three genes. Include gene-to-gene and gene-to-centromere distances.

a+ × +b:	I	II	III	IV	V	VI	VII
	a+	ab	a+	a+	a+	a+	ab
	a+	ab	+b	ab	++	+b	++
	+b	++	ab	++	ab	a+	++
	+b	++	++	+b	+b	+b	ab
	32	30	10	18	7	2	1
TOTAL = 100							

	I	II	III	IV	V	VI	VII
a+ × +c:	a+	ac	a+	a+	a+	a+	ac
	a+	ac	+c	ac	++	+c	++
	+c	++	ac	++	ac	a+	++
	+c	++	++	+c	+c	+c	ac
	69	3	5	8	12	3	0

TOTAL = 100

4. If gene q is 12 map units from the centromere, in a cross of q × +, what percent of the asci will show second division segregation?

5. Consider the following cross in a fungus that produces ascospores.

	PD	NPD	TT
a+ × +b	48	52	0
a+ × +c	90	1	9
a+ × +d	51	49	0
b+ × +d	60	10	30

   a. Which genes are linked?

   b. For linked genes, calculate gene-to-gene distance.

6. If genes a and b are linked by 2 m.u., how many tetratypes do you expect among 100 asci from a cross of a+ × +b?

7. In *Neurospora,* a cross of *ad trp* × ++ yielded the following ordered tetrads:

I	II	III	IV
ad trp	ad +	ad trp	ad trp
ad trp	ad +	ad +	+ trp
+ +	+ trp	+ trp	ad +
+ +	+ trp	+ +	+ +
126	6	30	18

V	VI	VII
ad trp	ad +	+ trp
+ +	+ trp	+ +
ad trp	ad +	ad trp
+ +	+ trp	ad +
6	2	12

   a. Determine gene-to-centromere distance.

   b. If the genes are linked, calculate the gene-to-gene distance and derive a map.

8. Three distinct traits, x, y, and z, were involved in a cross of *Neurospora*. From a cross of x ++ × +y z, the following ordered tetrads were recovered. Based on the data, construct a map of all three genes; be sure to indicate centromeres.

I	II	III	IV
x + +	x + +	x + +	x + +
x + +	+ y z	x y z	x + z
+ y z	x + +	+ + +	+ y +
+ y z	+ y z	+ y z	+ y z
68	70	18	14

V	VI	VII	VIII
x + +	x + +	x + z	x + z
+ y z	+ y z	+ y z	+ y +
x y z	x + z	+ y +	x + +
+ + +	+ y +	x + +	+ y z
4	4	2	6

9. In yeast, the distance from a to b is 12 and from a to c is 28. Calculate the distribution of PD, NPD, and TT if in a cross of:

   a. a+ × +b, TT/NPD = 4.

   b. a+ × +c, TT/NPD = 6.

10. A cross between two genes yielded equal numbers of PD and TT, and 12 times as many TT as NPD. What is the distance between genes?

Chapter 9

Bacterial Genetics

A. A high frequency of co-transformation (co-transduction) usually means the two genes are very close together.

EXAMPLE: In a transformation experiment, $x^+ y^+ z^+$ is used as the donor and $x^- y^- z^-$ as the recipient. Two hundred fifty x^+ transformants are selected, then replica plated to determine whether y^+ and/or z^+ are present. The genotypes of the transformants appear below. What can you conclude about the relative position of the genes?

$x^+ y^- z^-$	53
$x^+ y^- z^+$	173
$x^+ y^+ z^-$	7
$x^+ y^+ z^+$	17

We see that 76 percent of the colonies are $x^+ z^+$. This result suggests that x and z are close together. We see that y appears with x in only 10 percent of the colonies, suggesting that y is far away from x, and possibly unlinked. To calculate recombination frequency between x and z, we look at all of the times x^+ and z^+ appear apart ($x^+ y^- z^-$ and $x^+ y^+ z^-$).

$$RF = 60/240 = .25 \text{ m.u.}$$

B. Co-transformation (co-transduction) of non-linked genes requires two sets of exchanges.

Consider two genes, a and b, sufficiently far apart to be carried on separate DNA molecules ____a^+____ and ____b^+____. In order for transformants to be $a^+ b^+$, both pieces of DNA must be integrated into the recipient. This process requires two sets of breaks, and is equivalent to a double crossover; hence it will be rare.

Note that if a and b are close together and carried on one piece of DNA, only one set of breaks is required.

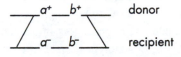

EXAMPLE: Consider the following co-transduction frequencies:

A and B	73 percent
A and C	7 percent
B and C	6 percent

Which, if any, gene(s) is (are) unlinked?

We notice that *C* appears rarely with either *A* or *B*. Gene *C* is probably unlinked to the other two genes.

C. To order genes in transformation/transduction, look for the order that predicts the observed double exchanges.

EXAMPLE: When $a^+ b^+ c^-$ is the donor and $a^- b^- c^+$ is the recipient, the least frequent class has the genotype $a^+ b^+ c^+$. What is the order?

Assume the order is *a b c;* then we can diagram the cross as:

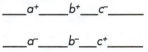

A double crossover produces $a^+ b^- c^-$; this class is not the least frequent. Hence, *b* is not in the middle. Try *c* in the middle.

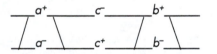

The dco produces $a^+ b^+ c^+$. This class is the lowest and thus *c* is in the middle.

D. In conjugation, a gene with a high frequency of transfer is closer to the origin of transfer.

EXAMPLE: A mating between his^+, leu^+, thr^+, pro^+, *str* sensitive cells and his^-, leu^-, thr^-, pro^-, *str* resistant cells is allowed to continue for 25 minutes. At this time the mating is stopped and the genotypes of the recombinants are determined. The results appear below. What is the first gene to enter and what is the probable gene order?

Genotype	Number of colonies
his^+	0
leu^+	12
thr^+	27
pro^+	6

We see that cells with thr^+ are the most frequent. The chance of the conjugation tube breaking increases with the length of time of the mating. Therefore, genes far from the origin of transfer will appear less frequently. We can order the genes merely based upon the frequency of genotypes seen. The order must be *thr leu pro his.* Since we see no his^+, and since we stopped the mating at 25 minutes, *his* must be after 25 minutes on the time map.

E. Viral genes can usually be ordered by a manner similar to establishing a map in eukaryotes.

EXAMPLE: *E. coli* is mixedly infected with two types of T4 phage: $r^+ m^+ tu^+$ and *r m tu*. The following progeny appear.

+ + +	1243
+ + tu	322
r m +	284
r m tu	1158
+ m +	175
+ m tu	54
r + +	58
r + tu	160
TOTAL	3454

Calculate the gene-to-gene distances and draw a map.

For *r–m,* look for those classes in which r^+m^+ are not together.

RF *r–m* = (175 + 54 + 58 +160)/3454 × 100 = 13

Similarly, RF *r–tu* = (322 + 284 + 54 + 58)/3454 × 100 = 21

RF *m–tu* = (322 + 284 + 175 + 160)/3454 × 100 = 27

These results suggest a map that looks like this:

__m____13 ___r_____21_____tu__

To check this, determine double crossovers as r^+ *m tu* and *r* mu^+ tu^+. We see that only the *r* alleles have been switched from the parental arrangement, so *r* is in the middle.

F. Lack of complementation usually means that the two mutants are in the same gene.

Consider the following two alternatives:

In case I, both DNA molecules make a nonfunctional protein. The cell has no normal protein, suggesting that it has a mutant phenotype. In case II, the top DNA has a good gene 2 and the bottom DNA has a good gene 1. This cell will have both good proteins 1 and 2, and will appear to be normal. Growth, or complementation, indicates that the mutants are in different functional units or genes.

EXAMPLE: Consider the following complementation data. How many genes are involved in the mutant phenotype, and which mutants are in which genes? (+ = complementation and – = no complementation)

	1	2	3	4	5
1	–	+	+	–	+
2		–	–	+	+
3			–	+	+
4				–	+
5					–

Look for those combinations in which no complementation occurs. These classes will give you mutations that are in the same gene. 1 and 4 don't complement and hence are in the same gene *(A)*. By a similar argument, 2 and 3 are in a different gene *(B)*. Mutant 5 complements with all the other mutants, and hence must be in a gene different than the one containing either 1,4 or 2,3 *(C)*.

G. If a mutant fails to complement mutations in two different genes, the new mutant is most likely a deletion.

EXAMPLE: Consider the new mutant 6 along with the mutants in concept F. It gives the following complementation results. What is the nature of mutant 6?

	1	2	3	4	5
6	–	+	+	–	–

We see that mutant 6 fails to complement 1 and 4, suggesting that mutant 6 is in gene *A*. But 6 also fails to complement mutant 5, which we know is in a separate gene. Mutant 6 affects both the gene for mutants 1 and 4 but also the gene for mutant 5. These results indicate the mutant is in two different genes. One explanation for this observation is a deletion that spans the regions covered by the strain with mutants 1 and 4 and with the strain with mutant 5. Alternatively, mutant 6 could be a double mutant, with one defect in one of each of two genes.

H. If two deletions are missing part of the same material (i.e., they overlap), they cannot give wild-type recombinants.

Consider the following two possibilities:

a. two deletions do not overlap:

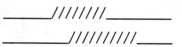

Recombination yields:

————/////////__//////// and _____

b. two deletions overlap:

————//////// _____
————///////// ____

Recombination yields all DNAs with some material deleted.

EXAMPLE: The following deletion strains are crossed and wild-type recombinants are selected. The results follow (+ = w.t. recombinants are recovered, – = no w.t. recombinants). Determine the order of the deletions.

	1	2	3
1	–	+	–
2	+	–	–
3	–	–	–

We see that strain 3 doesn't give any wild-type recombinants; it must span at least part of the region deleted in strains 1 and 2. Deletions 1 and 2 give wild-type recombinants, so they do not overlap. A possible map is:

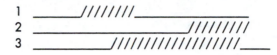

I. If a point mutation gives + recombinants when crossed to a deletion, the point mutation is outside the area covered by the deletion.

Consider the following cross between a deletion and a point mutation.

Case 1: point mutation is outside of deletion

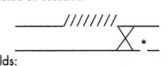

Recombination yields:

_____/////////_____*__ double mutant and _____ normal

Case 2: mutation is inside area covered by deletion

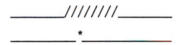

Recombination cannot occur within the area of a deletion; all recombinants are still mutant.

EXAMPLE: Point mutants 1, 2, and 3 are crossed with deletions *a* and *b,* and wild-type recombinants are selected. Based on the results below, what is the location of each point mutant? (+ = wild-type recombinants, – = no wild-type recombinants)

	1	2	3
a	+	–	+
b	–	+	+

Mutant 1 gives no wild-type with *b*; therefore it is located within the area covered by *b*. Similar logic places mutant 2 within the area deleted in *a*. Since mutant 3 gives wild-type with both deletions, it must be outside both deletions.

J. Polar mutations or mutations in the control region may give false negatives in complementation tests.

Polar mutations eliminate the function of distal genes in an operon.

EXAMPLE: Consider an operon of three genes in the order *A C B*. A partial diploid of the genotype *a⁻ (polar) b⁺ c⁺/a⁺ b⁻ c⁺* is constructed. What is the phenotype of this strain?

The polar mutation *a⁻* effectively makes the first DNA *a⁻ b⁻ c⁻*. The second strain is phenotypically *b⁻*. The partial diploid is thus *b⁻/b⁻* and hence mutant (see concept 9-F).

K. Deletions usually do not revert.

If a mutation is caused by a missense mutation, the altered base can change to the normal base. This situation will not occur if a number of bases is missing.

EXAMPLE: Five *trp⁻* mutants, 1 through 5, are plated on minimal medium. A few colonies appear for strains 2 and 5. What is the nature of each mutation?

The few colonies almost certainly represent reversions, so strains 2 and 5 must be point mutations. Strains 1, 3, and 4 are probably deletions.

L. Suppressible "revertants" should be separable by recombination.

Revertants fall into two classes: true revertants and second-site mutations that suppress or compensate for the original mutation.

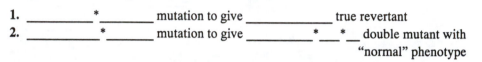

When each of these two strains is crossed to wild-type, different results appear.

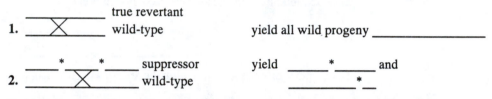

Both of the recombinants in the second case are still mutant. Note that this situation will hold either if the second mutation is within the original gene or located in a totally separate gene. The original mutant will be recovered in either case.

EXAMPLE: Three *leu⁻* revertants, *r1, r2,* and *r3,* are recovered. Each revertant is crossed to wild-type and the progeny are scored. Revertants 1 and 3 fail to yield wild-type progeny. What is the nature of each revertant?

Since revertants 1 and 3 fail to give wild-type recombinants, they each must contain a second-site "suppressor" mutation. Revertant 2 is a true revertant.

Summary

1. In transformation (transduction), gene order can be determined by considering double exchanges.
2. Events requiring two sets of exchanges will be rare.
3. In conjugation, we can order genes by looking at the frequency of appearance of different markers.
4. Lack of complementation suggests polar mutants, or mutants within the same gene.
5. Deletions do not revert or give wild-type recombinants when crossed to point mutants.
6. Deletions and point mutations can be ordered based on the appearance of wild-type progeny.

Practice Problems

1. **a.** In a transformation experiment, the donor is *ara⁺ nic⁺ gal⁺* and the recipient is *ara⁻ nic⁻ gal⁻*. *Ara* transformants are selected and then further tested. Forty percent were *ara⁺ gal⁺* and five percent were *ara⁺ nic⁺*. In what two possible orders are the genes arranged?

    b. You can do only one more transformation to determine gene order. You must use the same donor and recipient, but you can change the selection procedure for the initial transformants. What do you do and what results do you expect for each order you proposed?

2. DNA from a strain that is $a^+ \, b^+ \, c^+$ is used to transform a strain that is $a^- \, b^- \, c^-$. The numbers of each transformed genotype appear below. What can be said about the relative position of the genes?

Genotype	Number
$a^+b^-c^-$	312
$a^-b^+c^-$	320
$a^-b^-c^+$	308
$a^+b^-c^+$	16
$a^+b^+c^+$	11
$a^+b^+c^-$	140
$a^-b^+c^+$	21

3. Two *Hfr* strains 1 and 2 that are $a^+b^+c^+d^+e^+$ are mated to an F⁻ strain that is $a^-b^-c^-d^- e^-$. The matings are interrupted every five minutes, and the genotypes of the recombinants determined. The results appear below.

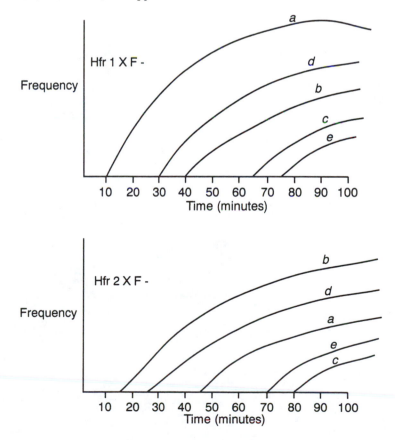

Draw one map that includes all genes and both F factors. Indicate F factors with boxes and the direction of transfer by arrows. On the standard map, gene *b* is located 20 minutes from the origin.

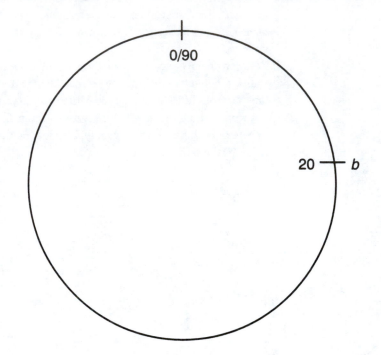

4. Eight independent *trp⁻* mutants are isolated. Complementation tests are performed in all pairwise combinations. Based on the results, determine how many genes you have identified, and which mutants are in which genes. (+ = complementation, – = no complementation)

	1	2	3	4	5	6	7	8
1	–	+	–	–	+	+	+	–
2		–	+	+	–	+	+	+
3			–	–	+	–	–	–
4				–	+	+	+	–
5					–	+	+	+
6						–	–	+
7							–	+
8								–

5. The following *Hfr* strains donate genes in the following order:

Strain	Order of transfer (first gene to enter is on right)
1	A C T E R
2	U I R E T
3	M B A C T
4	A B M U I

Determine the order of the genes on the chromosome.

6. You have isolated two *rII* mutants, *rII-1* and *rII-2,* in the T4 phage. *rII-1* gives no wild-type revertants, and mutant *rII-2* yields 4 revertants, 2 *reva,* 2 *revb,* 2 *revc,* 2 *revd.* Each revertant is crossed to wild-type with the following results (+ = wild-type recombinants recovered).

reva	+
revb	–
revc	–
revd	+

a. What is the nature of *rII-1* and *rII-2?*
b. What is the nature of each of the revertants?

7. In a transduction experiment, the donor is $d^+\ e^+\ f^+$, the recipient is $d^-\ e^-\ f^-$, and selection was for f^+. The results appear below. Determine the gene order.

Genotype	Number of transductants
$d^+\ e^+\ f^+$	25
$d^+\ e^-\ f^+$	4
$d^-\ e^+\ f^+$	80
$d^-\ e^-\ f^+$	256

8. The *trp* operon in *E. coli* has the following order: __p__ E _D_ C _B_ A__ . You isolate three independent *trp⁻* mutants and make partial diploids of each with __p⁺__E⁺__D⁺__C⁻__B⁺__A⁺___ . None of the partial diploids can make tryptophan. What are three different possible locations of these mutants?

9. You have nine *his⁻* strains, three of which represent deletions and six of which represent point mutations. You plate all nine strains on minimal media and score for growth. (+ = growth)

1	2	3	4	5	6	7	8	9
+	–	+	+	–	+	–	+	+

Phage are grown on each of the nine strains, and are then used to transduce each of the deletion strains. Transductants from each cross are plated on minimal media and scored for growth (+ = growth of transductants). Based on the results, determine:
a. which strains are deletions
b. the relative position of each deletion with respect to the others
c. the relative positions of the six point mutations

	Strain								
	1	2	3	4	5	6	7	8	9
Deletion									
A	+	–	–	–	–	–	–	+	+
B	+	–	+	+	–	–	+	+	–
C	+	–	+	–	+	+	–	–	+

10. You have isolated a number of point mutations (*a–g*) for the *rII* region of the T$_4$ phage. Pairwise crosses give the following percent of wild-type plaques.

Cross	% wild-type	Cross	% wild-type
a × b	0.5	a × c	0.3
a × d	0.8	a × f	0.3
b × e	0.4	b × d	1.3
b × f	0.2	c × d	0.5
c × g	0.8	e × g	1.0
b × g	1.6	g × d	0.3

You also cross each point mutation with each of five deletions (1–5) and score for wild-type recombinants. The results appear below (+ = wild-type recombinants; – = no wild-type recombinants).

				Point mutant			
Deletion	a	b	c	d	e	f	g
1	–	+	–	+	–	+	+
2	+	+	–	–	+	+	–
3	–	–	–	+	–	–	+
4	+	+	–	–	+	+	+
5	+	+	–	–	–	+	+

a. Draw a map of the point mutations, giving distances.
b. Determine the positions of the deletions with respect to the point mutations.
c. Mutants *e* and *a* complement each other, and *e* is known to be in *rIIB*. Which point mutations are in *rIIA* and which are in *rIIB*?
d. Which combinations of deletions will yield wild-type recombinants?

11. You have three *lac⁻* mutants (*a–c*). You perform the following transductions and get the following number of wild-type colonies.

Donor	Recipient	# of wild-type
lac a⁻ pro⁺	lac b⁻ pro⁻	93
lac b⁻ pro⁺	lac a⁻ pro⁻	27
lac a⁻ pro⁺	lac c⁻ pro⁻	15
lac c⁻ pro⁺	lac a⁻ pro⁻	64
lac b⁻ pro⁺	lac c⁻ pro⁻	10
lac c⁻ pro⁺	lac b⁻ pro⁻	98

Determine the order of the *lac* mutations with respect to the *pro* gene.

12. Phage mutant 1 grows in bacterial strains *B* and *D*, and mutant 2 grows in *A* and *D*. Only wild-type phage will grow in strain *C*. Both strains are used to simultaneously infect *D*. The progeny phage are diluted 10^{-7} and plated on *D*; 200 plaques result. The progeny phage are diluted 10^{-6} and plated on strain *C*; 30 plaques result. What is the recombination between mutant 1 and 2?

Chapter 10

Molecular Mutations and the Genetic Code

A. When trying to determine the sequence of bases, always write down all possibilities for each codon.

EXAMPLE: A peptide has the following amino acid sequence:

ala-pro-ser-lys-gly-gly-trp

What RNA sequences are possible?

Write down all the possible codons. *X* can be any one of the four bases.

ala - pro - ser - lys - gly - gly - trp

GCX - CCX - UCX - AAA - GGX - GGX - UGG

AGU - AAG

AGC

Note that only the codon for *trp* is unambiguous and that *lys* has only two codons. The other amino acids have at least four codons. Looking at the code, note that *arg, ser,* and *leu* can have six codons.

B. Always consider the least number of changes necessary to produce the mutant.

Mutations are rare events, and usually only one base is changed, added, or deleted.

EXAMPLE: A particular protein has *gly* in a certain position. Four mutants are isolated, and instead of having *gly,* they have, respectively, *ala, arg, trp,* and *leu.* What are the possible codon assignments, and what codon is probably used for *gly?*

We can summarize the results in the following way:

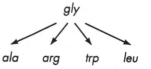

Now write down the possible codons.

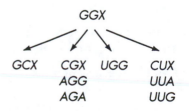

Work from the simplest to the most complex. *Trp* must be *UGG*. A single change of *GGG* to *UGG* probably occurred. Therefore, *gly* is probably *GGG*. Look next at *ala*, and see that a change of the second base of *gly* could give *ala*. Since *gly* is *GGG*, *ala* must be *GCG*. If *arg* is *AGG*, a change of *G* to *A* in the first position will give *AGG*. The *arg* codon can't be *AGA* because this would require two changes from *GGG*. *Arg* could also be *CGG*, but not *CG* (*U,A,C*). Thus, *arg* is either *AGG* or *CGG*. *Leu* is more baffling, for all *leu* codons differ from *gly* by at least two bases. Therefore, *leu* is either *CUG* or *UUG*. Alternatively, *leu* may have resulted from a frameshift mutation (see concept D).

C. If only one amino acid is changed, a missense mutation probably occurred.

EXAMPLE: A mutant of the peptide in concept A has the following sequence:

normal: *ala-pro-ser-lys-gly-gly-trp*
mutant: *ala-pro-ser-glu-gly-gly-trp*

What is the nature of the mutation?

We see that only one amino acid is changed: *lys* to *glu*. The simplest explanation is that the *lys* codon has mutated. Can a one-base change produce this result? *Lys* is *AAA* or *AAG*; *glu* is *GAA* or *GAG*. An *A* to *G* change in the first base could have produced this change.

D. A protein with more than one amino acid difference suggests that a frameshift (deletion or insertion) has occurred.

EXAMPLE: Consider the normal and mutant proteins below:

normal: *ala-pro-ser-lys-gly-gly-trp*
mutant: *ala-pro-ile-lys-gly-arg-leu*

What are the sequences of bases for each protein?

Look at the first changed amino acid (*ser* to *ile*) and also note that three amino acids are changed.

Ser:	*UCX*	*ile:*	*AUU*
	AGU		*AUC*
	AGC		*AUA*

We cannot go from any of the *ser* codons to the *ile* codons by a single base change. Inserting an *A* in front of the *ser* codon *UCX* gives *AUCX*, and *AUC* codes for *ile*. Therefore the sequences are:

normal: *GCX CCX UCA AAG GGC GGC UGC*
mutant: *GCX CCX AUC AAA GGG CGG CUG C*

A check of the code reveals that the remaining amino acids in the mutant are consistent with the above assignment.

E. A protein with a normal but truncated amino acid sequence may indicate that one of the codons mutated to a stop codon.

EXAMPLE: A mutant of the normal peptide in concept A has the following sequence:

normal: *ala-pro-ser-lys-gly-gly-trp*
mutant: *ala-pro-ser*

What is the nature of the mutation?

The protein stops after *ser*, suggesting that the *lys* codon has changed to a stop. *Lys* is either *AAA* or *AAG*. A change in the first base to *U* would yield either *UAA* or *UAG*, both stop codons.

F. A longer-than-normal protein suggests a mutation in the stop codon.

EXAMPLE: Consider the following C-terminal sequences:

> normal: *ser-thr-lys-leu*
> mutant: *ser-thr-lys-leu-trp-tyr-gln*

What has happened?

The normal mRNA must have a stop codon (*UGA* or *UAG*) after the codon for *leu*. If the second or third base of the stop signal had changed (for example, A to G), a *trp* codon would have been produced. Alternatively, A G could have been added after the G in a *UGA* stop codon.

G. Mutations in the anticodon of a tRNA can produce changes in amino acid sequences.

The mutated tRNA will still carry the same amino acid as the original tRNA, but it may insert this amino acid at a different codon.

EXAMPLE: A mutation is found in the anticodon of a tRNA as indicated below:

> normal: 5′ *GUA* 3′
> mutant: 5′ *UUA* 3′

What amino acid will be inserted and where will it be inserted?

We must first determine which amino acid this tRNA carries. The sequence 5′ *GUA* is complementary to 3′ *CAU* 5′, or 5′ *UAC* 3′, a codon for tyrosine. Now write the complementary sequence for the new anticodon: 5′ *UUA* 3′. The new codon is 5′ *UAA* 3′, a stop codon. Tyrosine will be inserted at stops coded by *UAA*, and the proteins will be longer than normal.

Summary

1. Write down possible codons, then look for single base differences.
2. A change of one amino acid usually means a missense mutation, whereas a change of many amino acids usually means a frameshift mutation.
3. Shorter-than-normal proteins usually result from premature stop mutations.
4. Longer-than-normal proteins usually result from mutations in the stop codon.

Practice Problems

1. In sickle-cell hemoglobin, a *glu* is replaced by a *val*. What change probably occurred in the codon?
2. In mutant proteins that are longer than normal, the first additional amino acid is found to be only *gln, lys, glu, ser, leu, tyr, arg, trp, gly,* or *cys*. Why are only these amino acids found?

3. Consider the following normal sequence:

   gly-leu-arg-gln-cys-ile-phe

   and the following mutant proteins:
   a. *gly-leu-arg-gln·*
   b. *gly-leu-arg-arg-cys-ile-phe*
   c. *gly-phe-lys-thr-met-gln-ile*
   What is the nature of each mutation, and what is the sequence of the normal RNA?

4. Repeating polymers are used in an *in vitro* protein-synthesizing system. For each of the following polymers, predict the sequence(s) of amino acids that can be produced.
   a. (*UC*)
   b. (*UUC*)
   c. (*CAA*)
   d. (*AUA*)
   e. (*AUG*)

5. If the genetic code were read in an overlapping manner, with the ribosome shifting one base for each new codon, how many amino acids would be changed as the result of a single transition?

6. For each of the following nucleotide sequences, determine the amino acid sequence.
   a. 5′ *AUGCAGUGCAAUCCUGCA* 3′
   b. 5′ *AUGCAGUCCAAUCCUGCA* 3′
   c. 5′ *AUGUAGUGCAAUCCUGCA* 3′
   d. 5′ *AUGCAGCUGCAAUCCUGCA* 3′
   e. 5′ *AUGCAGUGUAAUCCUGCA* 3′

7. A normal protein has arginine in a particular position. Mutants are found to have the following single amino acid substitutions: *ile, thr, ser, gly.* What is the most likely codon for *arg?*

8. A tRNA has the anticodon sequence 5′ *CCC* 3′; a mutant tRNA has 5′ *CCG* 3′.
   a. What amino acid is carried by the normal tRNA? by the mutant tRNA?
   b. What codon will be recognized by the mutant tRNA, and what will the consequence be?

9. If a mutant is induced by a mutagen that causes frameshifts, can the mutant be reverted by a chemical that causes transitions?

10. Hydroxylamine is a mutagen that causes only C → T transitions at the DNA level. Can mutations that yield stop codons be reverted by hydroxylamine?

11. The enzyme thinkase has the following amino acid sequence for positions 25–33:

25	26	27	28	29	30	31	32	33
met-	ala-	phe-	ser-	his-	arg-	glu-	val-	leu

A mutant, induced by a mutagen that causes single base insertions or deletions, has a shorter protein of only 30 amino acids:

25	26	27	28	29	30
met-	ser-	leu-	tyr-	ser-	pro

The first 24 amino acids in the mutant protein are normal. A partial revertant of the mutant was induced by the *same* mutagen. It has the following sequence (amino acids 1–24 and 34 and over are normal):

25	26	27	28	29	30	31	32	33
met-	ser-	leu-	tyr-	ser-	pro-	trp-	val-	leu

What is the sequence of the normal RNA in this region?

Chapter 11

Gene Control

A. Mutations in control regions will usually affect only the DNA on which they are located (*cis* dominant).

Mutations in control regions, such as promoters and operators, will usually affect only the DNA that they are a part of; they will not affect regions that are located on other DNA molecules.

EXAMPLE: In an operon, $p\ a\ b\ c$ (p = promoter; a,b,c = structural genes), what will be the phenotype of a strain whose genotype is $p^-\ a^+\ b^+\ c^+$? (p^+ = functional promoter, p^- = defective promoter, a^+, b^+, c^+ = normal functioning gene.)

The promoter is defective, RNA polymerase cannot bind, and no RNA will be made. The operon will always be off.

EXAMPLE: In an operon, $p\ o\ r\ s\ t$ (p = promoter, o = operator, $r,\ s,\ t$ = structural genes), what will be the effect of a defective operator, o^c or o^-, in the following strain: $p^+\ o^-\ r^+\ s^+\ t^+$? (o^c, o^- = operator defects in which no repressor can ever bind to operator.)

Since the operator is defective, a good repressor cannot bind to it, so no regulation will occur. The operon will always be on.

B. Mutations in repressor elements can exert their effect on all DNAs in a cell (*trans* dominant).

Repressor molecules are capable of interacting with all DNA molecules in a cell, regardless of the DNA from which they were made.

EXAMPLE: In the following operon, r = repressor gene, p = promoter, o = operator, and a,b,c = structural genes. For the following genotypes, determine if the operon will be always on, always off, or regulated.

1. $r^-\ p^+\ o^+\ a^+\ b^+\ c^+$ > *always on*
2. $r^+\ p^-\ o^+\ a^+\ b^+\ c^+/r^-\ p^+\ o^+\ a^+\ b^+\ c^+$

In strain 1, the cell makes a nonfunctional repressor, and it will never bind to the operator. The operon will always be on. In strain 2, we must examine each DNA separately, then together. The top DNA will never make operon RNA because of the defective promoter. The bottom DNA alone will always make RNA because of the defective repressor. The top DNA can make a good repressor which can bind to both operators. Therefore, this strain will be regulated.

C. Defects in structural genes will affect only the DNA with the mutation.

EXAMPLE: Consider again the operon in concept B. Assume that the genes a,b, and c are required to synthesize an amino acid. Which of the following strains will be able to make the amino acid, and under what conditions?

1. $p^+ \, o^+ \, a^+ \, b^- \, c^+$
2. $p^+ \, o^+ \, a^- \, b^+ \, c^+ / p^+ \, o^+ \, a^+ \, b^- \, c^+$
3. $p^- \, o^+ \, a^+ \, b^+ \, c^+ / p^+ \, o^+ \, a^+ \, b^+ \, c^-$

Strain 1 will produce regulated RNA, but will always make a defective *b* product. Thus, it will never make the amino acid. Strain 2 will make the amino acid under regulated conditions. The top DNA will make good *b* and *c*, and the bottom DNA will make good *a* and *c*. Strain 3 will never make the amino acid. No RNA can ever be made from the top DNA, since it is p^-. The bottom DNA will make regulated RNA, but will always produce defective *c*. In both cases, we get no functional *c*, and hence no amino acid.

D. To determine phenotypes from genotypes, look at one DNA at a time and determine which situations will yield no RNA or functional enzyme.

EXAMPLE: The following genetic loci are involved in the *lac* operon:

z = structural gene for ß -galactosidase
i = repressor gene
o = operator

For the following genotypes, determine if the cell can make the enzyme and if so, under what conditions.

Genotype	ß -galactosidase (+ = present, – = no enzyme)	
	Lactose absent	Lactose present
1. $i^+ o^+ z^+$	Always on +	always on +
2. $i^+ o^+ z^- / i^- o^+ z^+$	–	+
3. $i^+ o^+ z^+ / i^+ o\sigma z$	–	+

Strain 1 makes an inactive repressor, so the operon is always on (+ +). For strain 2, the top DNA will never make a good *z* product but will make a good repressor. The good repressor can bind to both operators and hence regulate the operon (– +). For strain 3, no good *z* product will ever be made by the bottom DNA, so we can ignore it. The top DNA is normal, so the operon will be regulated (– +).

E. In repressible operons, an inactive repressor must bind with a co-repressor to become active.

EXAMPLE: The *trp* operon, a repressible system, has the following sequence:

$p \, o \, E \, D \, C \, B \, A \, // \, p \, R$
(p = promoter, o = operator, A–E = structural genes, R = unlinked gene for repressor)

If all genes are normal, under what conditions will the operon be off?

The repressor cannot bind the operator by itself. It first must combine with tryptophan to be active. Initially, the operon is on, and tryptophan is made. The tryptophan combines with the repressor, activating the repressor so it can bind to the operator and turn off the operon.

F. In many bacterial operons involved in amino acid synthesis, transcription may be stopped by attenuators that are sensitive to levels of the appropriate charged tRNA.

EXAMPLE: In the *his* operon, the absence of histidine results in the production of full-length operon mRNA. In the presence of small amounts of histidine, some short RNAs as well as full-length RNAs are made. In the presence of large amounts of histidine, little if any RNA is made. Explain these results.

In the absence of histidine the operon is on (see concept 11-E), and transcription continues through the operon. Small amounts of histidine will cause charged tRNA^{his} to bind to the attenuator region, producing some small RNAs. High levels of histidine will activate the repressor, allowing it to bind to the operator and completely turn off the operon.

G. In eukaryotes, enhancer sequences may modulate the amount of transcription of a given gene.

EXAMPLE: Numerous deletions, upstream of the promoter for a eukaryotic gene, are produced as indicated, and the amounts of RNA produced are quantified. If /// = deleted regions, account for the results.

```
        -150         -100 -75   -50 -25  p  gene      # of RNA molecules made
1 _____        100
2 //////////_____         100
3 _____/////////_____         10
4 _____//////////_____         50
5 _____///////_____        100
```

We see a reduction in transcription for deletions 3 and 4, suggesting that the region from -125 to -75 contains an enhancer. Since strain 3 reduces transcription the most, the enhancer probably lies between -125 and -90.

H. Active eukaryotic genes are usually sensitive to DNase I.

Transcriptionally active genes are probably spatially looser than non-transcribed genes, thereby making it easier for DNase I to attack the DNA.

EXAMPLE: DNA was isolated from liver, muscle, and erythroblasts (precursors to red blood cells), digested with DNase I, and the gene for ß-hemoglobin isolated. The results are indicated below (+ = presence of ß-globin gene, – = absence).

Tissue	Presence/absence of ß-globin
liver	+
muscle	+
erythroblast	–

Explain these results.

If a gene can be isolated after DNase I treatment, it is not active transcriptionally. We see that ß-globin is not transcribed in liver or muscle, but that it is in erythroblasts.

I. In eukaryotes, intervening sequences (introns) must be removed before mature RNA is produced.

If a mature RNA is hybridized to DNA for the gene that made the RNA, loops will appear in the DNA where introns exist. In the following diagram, _____ = DNA and ----- = RNA.

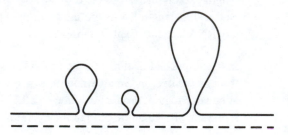

EXAMPLE: The gene for the enzyme thinkase is isolated and hybridized to cytoplasmic RNA for thinkase. The results appear below (_____ = DNA and ----- = RNA).

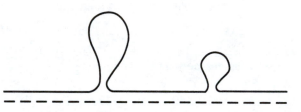

How many introns does the gene for thinkase contain?

We see two loops of DNA that do not have any complementary bases in the RNA. These loops must represent introns that were removed. Therefore, the gene appears to have two introns.

Summary

1. Regulatory proteins can bind to all DNAs in the cell.
2. Promoter and operator mutations will affect only the DNA to which they belong.
3. To determine phenotypes, begin by determining the phenotype for each DNA separately; then consider the effect of both DNA molecules.
4. Enhancer sequences are often far away from the gene(s) they influence.
5. Eukaryotic genes usually contain introns, and active genes are sensitive to DNase I.

Practice Problems

1. The following loci are involved in the *lac* operon.

   z = structural gene for β-galactosidase
   o = operator
   p = promoter
   i = repressor gene
   i^* = repressor that can't bind lactose, but can bind DNA

Fill in the table for each of the following genotypes.

	ß -galactosidase production (+ or –)	
Strain genotype	Lactose absent	Lactose present
1 $i^+p^+o^+z^-$	—	—
2 $i^+p^-o^+z^+$	—	~
3 $i^-p^+o^+z^+$	+	+
4 $i^+p^-o^+z^+/i^+p^+o^+z^-$	—	+/–
5 $i^+p^-o^-z^+/i^+p^+o^+z^-$	~	—
6 $i^*p^+o^+z^-/i^-p^+o^+z^+$	~	~

2. The symbols *a,b,* and *c* represent the gene for ß-galactosidase, the operator region, and the repressor of the *lac* operon, but not necessarily in that order. From the following data, determine which letter is the gene, the repressor and the operator. (+ = ß-galactosidase activity, – = no activity)

Strain Genotype	Lactose absent	Lactose present
1 $a^-b^+c^+$	+	+
2 $a^+b^+c^-$	+	+
3 $a^+b^-c^+$	–	–
4 $a^+b^-c^+/a^-b^+c^-$	+	+
5 $a^+b^+c^+/a^-b^-c^-$	–	+
6 $a^+b^+c^-/a^-b^-c^+$	–	+
7 $a^-b^+c^+/a^+b^-c^-$	+	+

(margin handwritten notes:
$o^+ z^+ I^+$
$o^+ z^+ I^-$
$o^+ z^- I^+$
$o^+ z^- I^+/o^- z^+ I^-$
$o^+ z^+ I^+/o^- z^- I^-$
$o^+ z^+ I^-/o^- z^- I^+$
$o^+ z^+ c$; $b\,z$; $a-I^-$ *)*

3. For the *lac* operon, write the genotype of a partial diploid that will produce ß-galactosidase by induction and permease under all conditions.

4. **a.** Provide two different types of mutations of the *lac* operon that would produce ß-galactosidase constitutively.
   b. How would each mutant behave in a partial diploid with wild-type?

5. You have identified a new, inducible operon with four adjacent regions in the order *PQRS*. The operon makes two enzymes, 1 and 2. Mutants in the following regions produce the following enzymes (+ = only in the presence of inducer, 0 = no enzyme, C = enzyme made constitutively).

Mutation	Enzyme 1	Enzyme 2
P^-	+	0
Q^-	0	+
R^-	0	0
S^-	C	C

a. Which regions are structural genes and which are regulatory regions?
b. Based on your answer to part a, predict the presence of enzymes 1 and 2 (+, 0, or C) in the following partial diploids:

case 1. $P^+ Q^- R^+ S^+/P^- Q^+ R^+ S^+$
case 2. $P^- Q^+ R^+ S^+/P^+ Q^- R^+ S^-$

6. The leader sequence near the attenuator of the *trp* operon contains the sequence 5′ *UGGUGG* 3′. What will be the consequence of changing this sequence to 5′ *AGGAGG* 3′?

7. A eukaryotic gene is 1.2 kilobases (kb) long. Deletions 0.5–0.7 kb downstream of the gene or point mutations 0.3–0.4 kb upstream of the gene each reduce the amount of mRNA made by 10-fold to 50-fold. Explain these results.

8. The tryptophan operon is a repressible operon, and the gene for the repressor is not encoded by the operon. The co-repressor is charged tRNA^{trp}, the gene for which is not part of the operon. For the following mutants, tell whether the enzymes of the operon will be made; then tell whether each mutant would be expected to be *cis* dominant in a partial diploid.

   a. RNA polymerase cannot bind the promoter.

   b. The repressor cannot bind to operator DNA.

   c. The repressor cannot bind charged tRNA^{trp}.

9. RNA-DNA hybrids are produced using mRNA for a given gene that is expressed in liver and bone marrow. The DNA used in each hybridization is full-length genic DNA. Based on the results below, provide an explanation for the different types of hybrid molecules. (_____ = DNA, - - - - - = RNA)

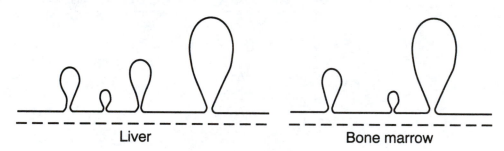

Liver   Bone marrow

10. A hypothetical operon has the sequence *A B C D E,* but the locations of the operator and promoter have not been identified. The gene for the repressor is found to be located far from the operon. Deletions of various parts of the operon are isolated and mapped. Their locations appear below.

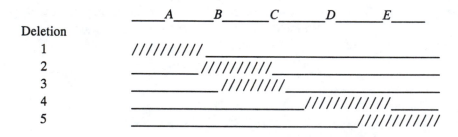

Deletions 2 and 3 are found to produce constitutive levels of RNA of the operon, and deletions 4 and 5 are found to never make RNA. Where are the operator and promoter probably located?

11. DNA from the following stages of development and adult tissues is digested with DNase I. The digested DNA is then tested for the presence of genes *A* and *B* (+ = presence of DNA for given gene; – = absence). Based on the results, what can be said about the activity of genes *A* and *B*?

	Fertilized egg	Gastrula	Neurula	Liver	Muscle	Bone marrow
Gene A	+	+	−	+	+	−
Gene B	−	−	+	−	+	+

12. The gene for an enzyme contains three introns. Cytoplasmic RNA from an individual lacking the enzyme is hybridized to full-length genic DNA. No loops are seen in the RNA-DNA hybrid. Explain these results.

13. Assume that failure to make insulin in diabetics could result from a defect in the promoter of the insulin gene or a deletion of the insulin gene. Devise an experiment to distinguish between these two alternatives.

Chapter 12

Molecular Biology and DNA Manipulation

A. If *A* does not equal *T,* or *G* does not equal *C,* the DNA is single-stranded.

EXAMPLE: From the following base percentages in specific DNA molecules, tell whether each is single- or double-stranded.

	A	*G*	*T*	*C*
DNA 1	32	18	31	19
DNA 2	17	28	31	24
DNA 3	29	25	29	17

Molecule 1 is double-stranded since *A = T* and *G = C*. Molecules 2 and 3 are single-stranded since *A* does not equal *T*, and *G* does not equal *C*.

B. The higher the *G-C* content, the higher the melting temperature.

Each *G-C* pair has three hydrogen bonds, which require more energy to disrupt than do the two hydrogen bonds of the *A-T* pair.

EXAMPLE: DNA molecule 1 melts at 74°C and molecule 2 melts at 81°C. What is the relative *G-C* content of each DNA?

Molecule 2 probably has the higher *G-C* content since it melts at a higher temperature.

C. A circular DNA molecule with *n* restriction sites will produce *n* fragments when digested.

EXAMPLE: When plasmid pBR322 is digested with *HaeI,* 11 fragments are produced. When it is cut with *BamHI,* one fragment is produced. How many restriction sites are there for each enzyme?

The first cut on a circle converts the circle to a line. The second cut will cut the line into two smaller lines. Therefore, there are 11 *HaeI* sites and one *BamHI* site.

D. A linear DNA molecule with *n* restriction sites will yield *n*+1 fragments.

EXAMPLE: A linear DNA molecule is cut with *EcoRI* and yields fragments of 3 kb, 4.2 kb, and 5 kb. What are the possible restriction maps?

There are three fragments (n+1), so there must be two restriction sites (n). The sites could be arranged in the following ways:

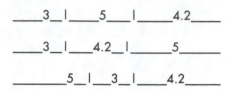

E. A mutation within a restriction site results in the loss of one or more fragments and the appearance of a new, larger fragment.

EXAMPLE: The DNA for a gene yields fragments of 1.7 kb, 2.1 kb, and 3.2 kb when digested with *BglII*. When DNA is isolated from a mutant that lacks the enzyme from this gene and is digested with *BglII*, fragments of 3.2 kb and 3.8 kb are seen. What has happened?

The mutation in the gene changed one or more bases in the site recognized by *BglII*, and the enzyme cut the molecule only once. The new fragment is the sum of 1.7 and 2.1, indicating that these two fragments are adjacent in the normal DNA.

F. A mutation that creates a new restriction site results in the loss of one fragment and the appearance of two new, smaller fragments.

EXAMPLE: Consider again the DNA in concept E. When DNA is isolated from a different mutant and digested with *BglII*, 1.3 kb, 1.7 kb, 1.9 kb, and 2.1 kb fragments appear. Explain these results.

We see that fragments 1.7 and 2.1 are present in both normal and mutant DNA. The site that generates these two fragments must still be intact in the mutant DNA. The remaining two fragments, 1.3 kb and 1.9 kb, add up to the missing 3.2 kb fragment. A new site within the original 3.2 kb fragment must have been created.

G. If a restriction fragment appears in both a digest from a single enzyme and from an enzyme mix, this fragment lacks a site for the second enzyme.

EXAMPLE: A linear molecule is digested as follows and yields the following fragments:

> *EcoRI:* 1.7, 2.1, 3.2 kb
> *HaeI:* 1.0, 1.4, 4.6 kb
> mix: 0.7, 1.0 1.4, 1.8, 2.1 kb

Which *EcoRI* fragments do not contain *HaeI* sites, and which, if any, *HaeI* fragments do not contain *EcoRI* sites?

The 2.1 kb *EcoRI* fragment also appears in the mix, and must therefore lack a *HaeI* site. The other *EcoRI* fragments disappear in the double digest, and must contain *HaeI* sites. Similarly, the 1.0 kb and 1.4 kb *HaeI* fragments must not contain an *EcoRI* site.

H. To derive a restriction map, consider fragments in the double digest that add up to a fragment from a single digest.

EXAMPLE: Refer again to the fragments in concept G. Derive a restriction map.

Since 1.0 + 0.7 = 1.7, and since 1.4 + 1.8 = 3.2, the 1.7 *EcoRI* fragment must have a *HaeI* site 1.0 kb from the end:

$$E\_\_1.0\_\_H\_\_\_0.7\_\_E$$

Similarly, the 3.2 fragment must have a *HaeI* site 1.8 kb from the end:

$$E\_\_\_1.8\_\_\_H\_\_\_\_1.4\_\_\_E$$

Now arrange possible orders for the *EcoRI* fragments:

```
____1.7____ |_____2.1_____ |_____3.2_____
____2.1_____1.7____ |_____3.2_____
____1.7___ |_____3.2_____ |____2.1__
```

Now include the known *HaeI* sites in the indicated fragments. If the order is:

```
        E      H      E      H
   2.1 ↓ 1.0 ↓ 0.7 ↓ 1.4 ↓ 1.8
```

we should have seen a 3.1 kb fragment in the single *HaeI* digest. If the order is 2.1, 0.7, 1.0, 1.4, 1.8, a *HaeI* digest should have produced a 2.8 kb fragment. Therefore the 1.7 kb *EcoRI* fragment is not in the middle. If the 3.2 kb fragment is in the middle, we should see either a 3.5 kb or 3.9 kb fragment in the *HaeI* digest. We didn't, so the 3.2 kb fragment is not in the middle. The order must be:

```
             E     E
             ↓     ↓
   1.7       2.1       3.2
_____
   1.0 ↑  0.7      1.8 ↑  1.4
       H                 H
```

If the *HaeI* site were 0.7 kb from the end, we should have seen a 0.7 kb fragment in the *HaeI* digest. A similar argument holds for the 1.8 kb fragment.

I. Cells that have taken up a plasmid should express the resistance associated with the plasmid.

EXAMPLE: In a typical transformation, much less than one percent of the cells will actually acquire the desired plasmid. How can you isolate cells that have the plasmid?

Construct a plasmid that contains one or more genes for resistance to antibiotics. Mix the cells with this plasmid and plate on a medium containing the antibiotic. Only the cells that have acquired the plasmid will grow.

J. The insertion of foreign DNA into a gene usually results in the loss of gene function.

EXAMPLE: A plasmid contains genes for resistance to ampicillin and tetracycline. The plasmid contains one site for a restriction enzyme, located within the tetracycline gene. The plasmid is treated with enzyme, mixed with foreign DNA, ligated, and incubated with *E. coli* cells. How do you isolate the cells that have the hybrid plasmid?

Plate the cells on a medium containing ampicillin, and collect all the cells that grow. Cells that have acquired a plasmid will have an intact ampicillin gene. Replica plate these cells to a medium containing tetracycline. Those cells that fail to grow in tetracycline will have the inserted gene. Go back to the original ampicillin plate and pick those cells that did not grow in tetracycline.

K. Radioactive RNA or cDNA can be used as probes because they will bind to fragments of DNA from which they were derived.

Such molecules will be complementary to DNA sequences and will form a detectable hybrid.

EXAMPLE: Human genomic DNA is digested with *EcoRI* and the fragments separated electrophoretically. The bands of DNA are transferred to a filter and incubated with radioactive cDNA for human insulin. The results appear below. (* = radioactive bands)

$$
\begin{array}{l}
\underline{\quad\quad} \\
\underline{\quad\quad} \\
\underline{\quad\quad}\,* \\
\underline{\quad\quad} \\
\underline{\quad\quad}\,* \\
\underline{\quad\quad}
\end{array}
$$

What can be concluded from this experiment?

The two labeled bands contain some sequences that are complementary to insulin cDNA, and presumably represent parts of the insulin gene. The presence of more than one band indicates that the gene contains an *EcoRI* site (see concepts 12-C and 12-D).

L. To determine the sequence of a DNA molecule, read up from the bottom of the gel.

EXAMPLE: A DNA molecule is sequenced by the Maxam-Gilbert method. From the gel below, determine the sequence of the DNA.

A	A+G	C	C+T
		—	—
		—	—
	—		
		—	—
			—
—	—		
		—	—
			—

The base at the 5′ end will be at the bottom of the gel. Since it appears in only the *C+T* column, it must be *T*. The next band appears in both *C* and *C+T* columns; it must be *C*. The overall sequence is 5′ *T C A T C G C C* 3′.

EXAMPLE: A DNA molecule is sequenced by the dideoxy method. Based on the gel below, what is the sequence in the *template* strand?

ddA	ddG	ddC	ddT
___			
		___	
			___
			___
	___		
___			
		___	
		___	

Read up from the bottom, remembering that the 5′ end will be at the bottom. Therefore, the sequence is 5′ *C C A G T T C A* 3′. This sequence is for a *newly* synthesized strand, so the template strand is 3′ *G G T C A A G T* 3′.

Summary

1. Single-stranded DNA molecules will have unequal amounts of A/T and/or G/C.
2. Melting temperature is proportional to G-C content.
3. Restriction maps can be determined by adding fragment sizes from double digests.
4. Mutations will alter the sizes of restriction fragments.
5. DNA inserted into a gene will usually destroy the function of the gene.
6. Radioactive RNA or cDNA can be used as probes for DNA sequences.
7. DNA sequences can be determined by reading up the gel.

Practice Problems

1. Two DNAs, *A* and *B*, have melting temperatures, respectively, of 73°C and 81°C. What can be concluded about the base composition of these two DNAs?
2. If a DNA molecule has $A/T=1.5$ and $G/C=1.0$, what is the nature of the DNA?
3. Determine if the following molecules are single- or double-stranded RNA or DNA.

Molecule percentage	A	T	G	C	U
1	27	26	23	24	0
2	33	17	21	29	0
3	33	0	21	29	17
4	21	0	29	29	21

4. The beginning portion of a gene is isolated and sequenced by the Maxam-Gilbert technique. The sequence appears on the following page.

A	A+G	C	C+T
		—	—
		—	—
	—		
		—	—
			—
—	—		
		—	
			—
—	—		
—	—		
	—		
			—
	—		
—	—		
		—	—
			—
	—		
—			
			—
			—

   a. What is the sequence of this strand? Be sure to indicate polarity.

   b. What is the sequence of RNA made from this strand?

   c. What are the first four amino acids in the protein?

5. If a DNA strand with the sequence 3′ *G C T G A A C G T C A G* 5′ is incubated with radioactive triphosphates and 10 percent dideoxy CTP, what sizes of labeled fragments will appear?

6. A linear DNA molecule cut with *PstI* yields fragments of 4.3 kb, 5.1 kb, and 6.6 kb. What three restriction maps are consistent with these results?

7. The DNA for a gene has the following restriction map for *BglII:*

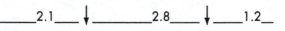

_____2.1___ ↓ _____2.8____ ↓ ____1.2__

What size fragments will be produced in a mutant in which:

   a. the site between the first two fragments is mutated?

   b. a new site is created 2.7 kb from the left end of the gene?

8. A pregnant 30-year-old woman learns that her father has Huntington's disease, an autosomal dominant disorder. There is no history of the disease in her husband's family. A DNA digestion test that reveals the presence of the allele for Huntington's is available. This test is performed on the woman's father, the woman, her husband, and the fetus. The results appear below.

Father	Husband	Woman	Fetus
—	—	—	—
—	—	—	—
—	—	—	—
—		—	

    a. Will the woman develop the disease?

    b. Will the woman's child develop the disease?

9. Digestion of a linear DNA with enzymes A and B yields the following fragments (in kb):

    A: 1.1, 2.0, 2.7, 3.2

    B: 1.5, 3.5, 4.0

    mix: 0.3, 0.8, 1.1, 1.2, 2.7, 2.9

Which of the following maps are inconsistent with the above results?

(a) (b) (c)

10. A DNA molecule is cut with *EcoRI* to yield one 16 kb fragment. When the original molecule is cut with *BglII,* fragments of 4.3 kb, 5.5 kb, and 6.2 kb are produced. When the molecule is digested with both enzymes, fragments of 2.7 kb, 3.5 kb, 4.3 kb, and 5.5 kb result.

    a. What is the physical nature of the DNA?

    b. Derive a restriction map.

11. A gene 4.2 kb long is inserted into the single *EcoRI* site of a 7.4 kb plasmid. The plasmid is then digested with *HindIII* and yields fragments of 3.8 kb, 4.9 kb, and 2.9 kb. A digestion with both *EcoRI* and *HindIII* produces fragments of 1.1 kb, 1.4 kb, 1.5 kb, 2.7 kb, and 4.9 kb. Which fragments contain information for the gene?

12. A 3.0 kb piece of human DNA is mixed with a 7.0 kb plasmid that has been opened by the same enzyme that produced the human fragment. The molecules are then separated by electrophoresis. Bands corresponding to molecules 3, 6, 7, 10, and 14 kb are seen.

    a. Explain these results.

    b. Which molecule(s) should be used to transform cells?

13. A 6.0 kb plasmid contains genes for ampicillin, tetracycline, and chloramphenicol resistance. It also contains singles sites for *EcoRI, BglII, SmaI,* and *PstI.* A mouse oncogene is separately inserted into each of the restriction sites. The resultant hybrid molecules are used to transform *E. coli,* and the transformants scored for resistance to antibiotics. The results appear below (R = resistant, S = sensitive).

Enzyme	Ampicillin	Tetracycline	Chloramphenicol
EcoRI	R	R	R
BglII	R	R	S
SmaI	R	S	R
PstI	S	R	R

a. Draw a map of the plasmid that shows the site of each enzyme.
b. The plasmid, without any foreign DNA, is digested with the following enzyme mixtures; the following fragments (in kb) are produced:

EcoRI + SmaI	0.8, 5.2
EcoRI + BglII	1.3, 4.7
EcoRI + PstI	2.5, 3.5
EcoRI + SmaI + BglII	0.8, 1.3, 3.9
EcoRI + SmaI + PstI	0.8, 1.7, 3.5

Redraw your map from (a) and include the distances.

14. A linear DNA molecule is labeled with ^{32}P at its 5′ ends. It is then digested to yield the following fragments (* = labeled fragments):

HindIII:	3.0*, 4.0, 5.0*
BglII	1.8*, 2.2*, 2.7, 5.3
mix	1.2, 1.5, 1.8*, 2.2*, 2.5, 2.8

Draw a restriction map.

15. DNA from mouse embryos and adult lymphocytes is digested with a restriction enzyme and probed with radioactive cDNA for the light chain of the antibody molecule. The labeled fragments appear below.

Embryo	Lymphocyte

Explain these results.

Chapter 13

Allele Frequency and Hardy-Weinberg Equilibria

A. If two alleles produce three distinctive phenotypes, the frequency of one allele can be calculated as: frequency of the homozygote + ½ (frequency of heterozygotes).

EXAMPLE: In a group of 200 humans, 160 had blood type MM, 36 were MN and 4 were NN. What is the frequency of the N allele? Of the M allele?

First calculate the frequency of each genotype as follows:

$$\text{freq (MM)} = {}^{160}/_{200} = 0.8$$
$$\text{freq (MN)} = {}^{36}/_{200} = 0.18$$
$$\text{freq (NN)} = {}^{4}/_{200} = 0.02$$

Now use the above relationship to calculate the allele frequency for N. Call this frequency q.

$$q = 0.02 \times \text{½ (0.18)} = 0.02 + 0.09 = 0.11$$

The frequency of M, (or p) =

$$0.8 + \text{½ (0.18)} = 0.8 + 0.09 = 0.89$$

With only two alleles, if the frequency of one allele is known, then the frequency of the second allele is 1 – (frequency of first allele), or in general terms $p + q = 1$.

The allele frequencies could also have been determined by counting the alleles directly. A population of 200 individuals will have 400 alleles at each given locus.

$$\text{freq of M (or } p) = [(160 \times 2) + 36]/400 = (320 + 36)/400 = 356/400 = 0.89$$

Similarly,

$$\text{freq of N (or } q) = [(4 \times 2) + 36]/400 = (8 + 36)/400 = 44/400 = 0.11$$

B. If a population is at equilibrium, the distribution of genotypes should be: p^2 (A$_1$ A$_1$) + 2 pq (A$_1$ A$_2$) + q^2 (A$_2$ A$_2$).

If the chance of a gamete getting A$_1$ equals p, then the chance of getting both A$_1$ alleles equals $p \times p = p^2$. A similar argument holds for q. There are two ways that a heterozygote could arise; hence 2 pq.

EXAMPLE: Assume that in a given human population the frequency (p) of the tongue curling allele is 0.4. What are the expected genotypic frequencies at equilibrium?

Since $p = 0.4$, $q = 1 - p = 0.6$. Therefore, we expect

$$(0.4)^2 \, CC + 2 \, (0.4) \, (0.6) \, Cc + (0.6)^2 \, cc = 0.16 \, CC + 0.48 \, Cc + 0.36 \, cc$$

Note that if a recessive allele is frequent, homozygous recessive individuals are numerous and the number of homozygous individuals may exceed the expected ratio from a single cross.

EXAMPLE: Which of the following populations are in Hardy-Weinberg equilibrium?

Population	$A_1 A_1$	$A_1 A_2$	$A_2 A_2$
1	0.25	0.5	0.25
2	0.60	0.2	0.2
3	0.04	0.32	0.64

We first have to calculate allele frequencies for each population.

For 1, $p = 0.25 + \frac{1}{2} (0.5) = 0.5$; $q = 0.5$ since $q = 1 - p$.
For 2, $p = 0.6 + \frac{1}{2} (0.1) = 0.7$; $q = 0.3$
For 3, $p = 0.04 + \frac{1}{2} (32) = 0.2$; $q = 0.8$

Now use the allele frequencies to predict expected genotypic ratios. In 1, we expect $(0.5)^2 \, (A_1 A_1)$ or $0.25 \, (A_1 A_1)$; $2 \, (0.5) \, (0.5) = 0.5 \, (A_1 A_2)$ and $(0.5)^2 \, A_2 A_2 = 0.25 \, A_2 A_2$. The observed fits the expected ratio, so the population is probably in equilibrium.

For 2, we expect $(0.7)^2 \, A_1 A_1$ or $0.49 \, A_1 A_1$; $0.2 \, (0.7) \, (0.3) \, A_1 A_2$ or $0.42 \, A_1 A_2$; and $(0.3)^2 \, A_2 A_2$ or $0.09 \, A_2 A_2$. You could run a chi-square, but the deviation from expected is so large, it is not necessary. We see much deviation from expected (0.42 vs. 0.2) for heterozygotes. The population is probably not in equilibrium.

For population 3, $0.04 \, A_1 A_1$; $0.32 \, A_1 A_2$; and $0.64 \, A_2 A_2$ is expected. Since these frequencies match the expected, the population is in equilibrium.

C. If a population is at Hardy-Weinberg equilibrium, the frequency (q) of a recessive allele can be calculated as $\sqrt{\text{frequency of recessive phenotype}}$.

Since q^2 = frequency of recessive phenotype, q = the square root of the frequency.

EXAMPLE: In Black Americans the incidence of individuals with sickle-cell anemia is about one in 10,000. Calculate the allele frequencies.

Calculate $q = \sqrt{1/10,000} = 1/100 = 0.01$

Since $p + q = 1$ and $1 - q = p$,

$$p = 1 - 0.01 = 0.99$$

You could also calculate the expected frequency of heterozygous individuals as

$$2 \, pq = 2 \, (0.99) \, (0.01) = 0.0198$$

or about 2 percent.

D. If a population is at equilibrium, the frequency of an X-linked recessive allele (q) can be calculated as: number of affected males/total males.

Recall that males need only one copy of an X-linked recessive trait to have the trait.

EXAMPLE: In an island population of 50 males and 50 females, two of the males are color-blind. What is the frequency of the color-blind allele? What is the frequency of females that are carriers?

The frequency of affected males is $2/50 = 0.04$. Thus q, the frequency of the color-blind allele, is 0.04. Since $p + q = 1$, $p = 0.96$. Thus, the frequency of carrier females is

$$2\,pq = 2\,(0.96)\,(0.04) = 0.0768$$

or about eight percent.

E. If a population containing three alleles at one locus is at equilibrium, the distribution of genotypes should be p^2 (A$_1$ A$_1$) + 2 pq (A$_1$ A$_2$) + 2 pr (A$_1$ A$_3$) + 2 qr (A$_2$ A$_3$) + q^2 (A$_2$ A$_2$) + r^2 (A$_3$ A$_3$).

Since $p + q + r = 1$, the genotypes will be distributed as $(p + q + r)^2$.

EXAMPLE: The frequency among White Americans of the three alleles I^A, I^B, I^O of the ABO blood system are 0.28, 0.06, and 0.66, respectively. Calculate the frequencies of each blood type.

Let p = frequency of I^A, q = frequency of I^B, and r = frequency of I^O.

Type A blood results from genotypes $I^A I^A$ and $I^A I^O$; therefore the frequency of type A blood is $p^2 + 2\,pr = (0.28)^2 + 2\,(0.28)\,(0.66) = (0.0784) + (0.3696) = 0.4480$, or 45%.

For type B blood, $q^2 + 2\,qr = (0.06)^2 + 2\,(0.06)\,(0.66) = 0.0828$, or 8%.

For type AB blood, $2\,pq = 2\,(0.28)\,(0.06) = 0.0336$, or 3%.

For type O blood, $r^2 = (0.66)^2 = 0.4356$ or 44%.

F. A higher-than-expected frequency of homozygotes in a population suggests inbreeding.

Inbreeding causes an increase in homozygotes at the expense of heterozygotes.

EXAMPLE: The frequencies of genotypes A$_1$ A$_1$, A$_1$ A$_2$, and A$_2$ A$_2$ in an isolated population are 0.375, 0.25, and 0.375 respectively. Calculate the allele frequencies, determine if the population is in equilibrium, and, if not, explain why not.

Simple inspection will not tell us if the frequency of heterozygotes is lower than expected. We must first calculate the allele frequencies.

$$p(A) = 0.375 + \tfrac{1}{2}\,(0.25) = 0.375 + 0.125 = 0.5$$

Since $q = 1 - p$, q also = 0.5. If the population is in equilibrium, we expect 2 pq heterozygotes, or 2 (0.5) (0.5) = 0.50 or 50%, and $(0.5)^2 = 0.25$ for each homozygote. The population is not in equilibrium; heterozygotes are reduced at an expense of homozygotes. Inbreeding might explain these results, but see also chapter 14.

Note: Inbreeding may change the genotypic frequencies, but allele frequencies will remain unchanged.

G. If a proportion (*f*) of individuals in a population interbreed, the genotypic distribution can be calculated as $(p^2 + fpq)$ (A$_1$ A$_1$) + (2 *pq* − 2 *fpq*) (A$_1$ A$_2$) + $(q^2 + fpq)$ (A$_2$ A$_2$).

Individuals could be homozygous as a consequence of inbreeding, the *fpq* terms, or through random mating, the p^2 and q^2 terms.

EXAMPLE: In a population of flies, 20 percent of the individuals interbreed. If $q = 0.4$, what is the expected genotypic distribution?

Let $f = 0.2$, $q = 0.4$, and $p = 0.6$.

frequency of A$_1$ A$_1$ = $p^2 + fpq$ = 0.36 + 0.048 = 0.408

frequency of A$_2$ A$_2$ = $q^2 + fpq$ = 0.16 + 0.048 = 0.208

frequency of A$_1$ A$_2$ = 2 *pq* − 2 *fpq* = 0.48 − 0.096 = 0.384

H. The inbreeding coefficient can be calculated as: 1 − (observed heterozygote frequency/expected heterozygote frequency).

EXAMPLE: In a population of wild oats, the frequencies of homozygous dominant, heterozygous, and homozygous recessive individuals were 0.67, 0.06, and 0.27, respectively. What is the inbreeding coefficient?

First, calculate the allele frequencies.

$$p = 0.67 + \tfrac{1}{2} (0.06) = 0.7$$
$$q = 1 - p = 0.3$$

Now calculate the expected frequency of heterozygotes.

$$2 \, pq = 2 \, (0.3) \, (0.7) = 0.42$$
$$\text{Inbreeding coefficient} = 1 - (0.06/0.42) = 0.86$$

This number is a high inbreeding coefficient and suggests that most of the oats in this population reproduce by self-pollination.

Note: Another way to calculate the inbreeding coefficient is: (expected heterozygotes − observed heterozygotes)/expected heterozygotes.

Summary

1. Calculate allele frequencies as: frequency of homozygote + ½ (frequency of heterozygotes).
2. To estimate allele frequencies in cases of complete dominance, assume equilibrium and use q to represent recessive phenotype frequency.
3. Remember that the sum of all allele frequencies must equal 1.
4. Inbreeding reduces the expected number of heterozygotes.

Practice Problems

1. A particular human population has 300 *MM,* 180 *MN,* and 420 *NN* individuals. Calculate the allele frequencies and determine if the population is in equilibrium.

2. For the numbers in problem one, assume random mating occurs among the individuals. What will be the frequencies of each type of individual in the next generation?

3. In a human population of 200 people, 17 had type A blood, 52 type B, 3 type AB, and 128 type O. If this population is in equilibrium, what are the allele frequencies?

4. In a sample of 300 humans, there are 69 MM, 108 MN, and 123 NN. Calculate the inbreeding coefficient.

5. What allele frequency will generate:
   a. twice as many homozygous recessives as heterozygotes?
   b. six times as many homozygous recessives as heterozygotes?

6. About one in 20,000 people is born with cystic fibrosis. Assume that this trait is inherited as an autosomal recessive, even though recent research suggests a different mode of inheritance.
   a. What is the frequency of the cystic fibrosis allele?
   b. What percentage of the population is expected to be carriers?

7. Red-green color-blindness, a recessive X-linked disorder, affects about 64 out of 10,000 women.
   a. What are the allele frequencies?
   b. What percent of the men would be expected to have normal vision?

8. An X-linked recessive disorder is found in 1 percent of the males.
   a. What is the frequency of the recessive allele?
   b. What fraction of the females would be expected to be carriers?

9. If $p = 0.8$, $q = 0.2$, and $f = 0.4$, calculate the distribution of genotypes in the next generation.

10. In a large, randomly-mating human population, the frequencies of the I^A, I^B, and I^O alleles are 0.6, 0.3, and 0.1, respectively. Calculate the expected frequencies for each blood type.

11. If, in a population with two alleles at an autosomal locus, $p = 0.8$, $q = 0.2$, the frequency of heterozygotes is 0.20, what is the inbreeding coefficient?

12. Attack or defend mathematically the following statement: "Assume that yellow seeds in peas are the result of a dominant allele at one locus, and that the recessive color is green; with time, the frequency of yellow plants will increase, until about 3/4 of the individuals are yellow."

13. Shell color in the European snail is controlled by three alleles at a single locus: C^B (brown), C^P (pink), and C^Y (yellow). The brown allele is dominant to both pink and yellow; pink is dominant to yellow; yellow is completely recessive. In one population of snails the colors were distributed as follows:

Brown	472
Pink	462
Yellow	66
TOTAL	1000

If this population is in equilibrium, what are the allele frequencies?

14. In a particularly large human population, the frequencies of blood types were distributed as follows: 0.486 *MM,* 0.332 *MN,* and 0.182 *NN.*
   a. Calculate the allele frequencies.
   b. Determine if the population is in equilibrium.
   c. If it is not in equilibrium, calculate the inbreeding coefficient.

Chapter 14

Allele Frequencies as a Result of Mutation, Migration, and Selection

A. Mutations cause very small changes in allele frequency per generation.

Mutation rates per gene typically are between 10^{-4} and 10^{-6} per generation, and some are much less.

EXAMPLE: Consider a population in which all individuals are initially AA. If the forward mutation rate (μ) of $A \to a$ is 10^{-5}, what is the frequency of A after one generation?

Initially, $p = 1$. The frequency of A will be reduced by 0.00001 in one generation. Since $q = 0$ initially, there will be no reverse mutations. Therefore $p_1 = 1 - 0.00001 = 0.99999$.

B. For a gene with only two alleles, the change in frequency of an allele depends both on the forward mutation rate, μ, and the reverse rate, v: $\Delta p = vq - \mu p$ and $\Delta q = \mu p - vq$.

The forward mutation rate of $A \to a$ (μ) decreases the number of A alleles, and the reverse rate $a \to A$ (v) increases the number of A alleles.

EXAMPLE: Consider a population in which $p = 0.8$ and $q = 0.2$. If $\mu = 5 \times 10^{-5}$ and $v = 2 \times 10^{-5}$, what are the new allele frequencies after one generation?

$$\Delta p = vq - \mu p = (2 \times 10^{-5})(2 \times 10^{-1}) - (5 \times 10^{-5})(8 \times 10^{-1}) =$$
$$(4 \times 10^{-6}) - (40 \times 10^{-6}) = -3.6 \times 10^{-5}$$
$$\Delta q = \mu p - vq = (5 \times 10^{-5})(8 \times 10^{-1}) - (2 \times 10^{-5})(2 \times 10^{-1}) =$$
$$(40 \times 10^{-6}) - (4 \times 10^{-6}) = 3.6 \times 10^{-5}$$

Therefore $P_1 = 0.8 - 0.000036$ and $q_1 = 0.2 + 0.000036$

C. If only mutations are changing allele frequencies, the equilibrium frequency $\hat{q}$ is $\mu/(\mu + v)$ and the equilibrium frequency $\hat{p}$ is $v/(\mu + v)$.

EXAMPLE: Consider the situation in concept B, and calculate the equilibrium frequencies.

$$\hat{q} = \mu/(\mu + v) = 5 \times 10^{-5}/[(5 \times 10^{-5}) + (2 \times 10^{-5})] = 5 \times 10^{-5}/7 \times 10^{-5} = 0.71$$
$$\hat{p} = v/(\mu + v) = 2 \times 10^{-5}/[(5 \times 10^{-5}) + (2 \times 10^{-5})] = 2 \times 10^{-5}/7 \times 10^{-5} = 0.29$$

Note that equilibrium frequencies do not depend on original allele frequencies. Note also that this example is an idealized situation. Rarely is mutation the only factor influencing allele frequencies.

D. The recessive allele frequency after migration can be calculated as: original frequency – (fraction migrating × the difference in allele frequencies between the original and migrant population).

If the migrant population has a higher frequency than the original, q will increase. If the migrant population has a lower frequency than the original, q will decrease. Mathematically, this can be expressed as: $q' = q - m (q - q_m)$, where m = proportion of the migrant population moving.

EXAMPLE: In a population of 900 butterflies, the frequency of the fast allele of an enzyme (p) is 0.7 and of the slow form (q) is 0.3. Ninety butterflies from this population migrate to a population in which $q = 0.8$. What are the allele frequencies of the new population?

We first must calculate $m = 90/900 = 0.1$. Since $q = 0.8$ and $q_m = 0.3$,

$$q' = 0.8 - 0.1 \ (0.8 - 0.3) = 0.8 - 0.1 \ (0.5) = 0.8 - 0.05 = 0.75.$$

Since $q' + p' = 1$, $p' = 0.25$.

E. In a population composed of natives and migrants, the percentage of alleles contributed by the migrants is:

$$\frac{[\text{frequency in native } (q) - \text{frequency in mixed } (q')]}{[\text{frequency in native } (q) - \text{frequency in migrant } (q_m)]}$$

EXAMPLE: In a particular human population, the frequency of the M allele (p) is 0.75 and of the N allele (q) is 0.25. In the migrant population the frequency of N is 0.4. The mixed population has q equal to 0.32. What percent of the N alleles in the mixed population were derived from the migrant population?

Set up the equation:

$$m = (q - q')/(q - q_m) =$$
$$(0.25 - 0.32)/(0.25 - 0.4) = -0.07/-0.15 = 0.47 \text{ or } 47\%.$$

F. If different genotypes are differentially fit, the distribution of genotypes after selection will be: fitness × original frequency.

EXAMPLE: In a particular population, the frequency of $AA = 0.25$, $Aa = 0.5$ and $aa = 0.25$. If the fitnesses of these genotypes are 1, 0.8, and 0.5 respectively, calculate the frequency of genotypes and the allele frequencies after selection.

First calculate the frequencies of genotypes after selection:

$$AA = (1) \ (0.25) = 0.25$$
$$Aa = (0.8) \ (0.5) = 0.40$$
$$aa = (0.5) \ (0.25) = 0.125$$

Note that these numbers do not equal one, since some of the individuals are selected against. Frequency of a genotype = number/total. Therefore,

$$AA = 0.25/0.775 = 0.322$$
$$Aa = 0.4/0.775 = 0.516$$
$$aa = 0.125/0.775 = 0.162$$

We can now calculate allele frequencies from homozygote frequency + ½ (heterozygote frequency) (see chapter 13).

$$p(A) = 0.322 + ½ (0.516) = 0.322 + 0.258 = 0.58$$
$$q(a) = 0.162 + ½ (0.516) = 0.162 + 0.258 = 0.42$$

G. The allele frequency of a recessive allele after selection is $q_s = q(1 - sq)/(1 - sq^2)$, where s = selection coefficient.

EXAMPLE: The frequency of a slow-moving allele of an enzyme (q) was initially 0.7. If the selection coefficient is 0.6, what is the allele frequency one generation after selection?

$$q_s = q (1 - sq)/(1 - sq^2) = (0.7)[1 - (0.6) (0.7)]/[1 - (0.6) (0.7)^2] =$$
$$(0.7 - 0.42)/(1 - 0.294) = .28/.706 = 0.396$$

H. If a homozygous recessive genotype is completely lethal, the recessive allele frequency after one generation is $q/(1 + q)$.

EXAMPLE: In a population, a recessive allele was initially neutral and had a frequency of 0.3. The environment changed so that the homozygous recessive genotype became completely lethal. What is the expected frequency after one generation? After two generations?

$$q_1 = q/(1 + q) = 0.3/1.3 = .230$$

For the second generation, we must start with the new frequency.

$$q_2 = 0.23/1.23 = 0.187$$

Notice that it will take many generations to completely eliminate the allele. It will still be present in the heterozygotes.

I. If the heterozygote has an advantage over both homozygotes, the equilibrium frequency of the recessive allele, $\hat{q}$, should be $\dfrac{s_1}{(s_1 + s_2)}$, where s_1 = selection coefficient of homozygous dominant and s_2 = selection coefficient of homozygous recessive.

EXAMPLE: Individuals heterozygous for the sickle-cell hemoglobin allele have an advantage in areas where malaria is present. Individuals with sickle-cell disease usually die. If the selection coefficient of the homozygous normals is 0.2, what frequency of the sickle-cell allele do we expect at equilibrium?

Let s_2 = selection coefficient of Hb^s/Hb^s and s_1 = selection coefficient of Hb^A/Hb^A. Since sickle-cell individuals die, $s_2 = 1$. Therefore $\hat{q} = 0.2/(1 + 0.2) = 0.17$. Note that $\hat{p}$ will be $s_2/(s_1 + s_2) = 1/1.2 = 0.83$.

J. If both mutations and selection are operating, the equilibrium frequency of the recessive allele after selection is approximately $\sqrt{\mu / s}$ and μ/s for a dominant allele.

EXAMPLE: In corn, the mutation rate from the normal allele to the recessive sugary allele is 2.5×10^{-6} and the selection coefficient is 0.1. What is the expected equilibrium frequency of the sugary allele?

$$\hat{q} = \sqrt{2.5 \times 10^{-6}/10^{-1}} = .005$$

Note again that $\hat{q}$ does not depend on the original allele frequency.

Summary

1. Equilibrium allele frequencies depend on forward and reverse mutation rates and selection coefficients.
2. A migrant population with a higher allele frequency than the stable population will increase the allele frequency in the stable population; a lower frequency will decrease the allele frequency in the stable population.
3. The allele frequency of a recessive allele after selection is $q_s = q(1 - sq)/(1 - sq^2)$.
4. For a homozygous recessive lethal, the allele frequency after one generation is $q/(1 + q)$.
5. Heterozygotes will be maintained in a population if they have an advantage over both homozygotes.

Practice Problems

1. A test tube of *E. coli* contains 10^{11} cells, all of which are sensitive to infection by T1 phage. If the mutation rate to resistance is 3×10^{-8}, how many resistant cells do you expect after one generation?
2. In a large population of *Drosophila*, the frequency of the *ebony* allele *(e)* is 0.32. If $e^+ \rightarrow e$ is 2×10^{-5} and $e \rightarrow e^+$ is 10^{-6}, calculate:
   a. the allele frequencies after one generation.
   b. the equilibrium allele frequencies.
   c. the equilibrium allele frequencies if the *ebony* allele has a fitness of 0.9.
3. If $A \rightarrow a$ is five times $a \rightarrow A$, what will the equilibrium frequency of *a* be? Repeat the above calculation for: $(A \rightarrow a)/(a \rightarrow A) = 10$ and $(A \rightarrow a)/(a \rightarrow A) = 2$.
4. The frequency of an allele of the Duffy blood group locus in Caucasians is 0.429. The frequency of this allele in a Black California population is 0.094. The allele is not found in Black Africans. What proportion of the alleles in the American Black population is derived from Caucasians?
5. In a particular human population, 16 percent of the people have blue eyes. Twenty percent of this population migrates to a population in which only nine percent of the individuals are blue-eyed. If we assume that blue eyes are inherited as an autosomal recessive trait, what is the frequency of the blue allele in the new population?
6. The genotypes *AA, Aa,* and *aa* are equally frequent in a population. If the fitnesses of the genotypes are respectively 1.0, 0.8, and 0.3, and if mutations are negligible, what are the genotypic distributions and allele frequencies in the next generation?
7. Two alleles for transferrin, Tf^A and Tf^B, are found in pigeons. Eggs from heterozygous females are more resistant to bacterial infection than eggs from either homozygote. If the selection coefficient of eggs from Tf^A/Tf^A is 0.31 and 0.22 for Tf^B/Tf^B, what equilibrium frequency of the alleles do you expect?
8. The frequency of a recessive allele *b* is 0.2 and the selection coefficient is 0.8. Calculate the allele frequencies after one and two generations.
9. If the frequency of an allele *d* is 0.25 in a migrant population and 0.5 in a mixed population, and if the migration rate is 0.1, what is the frequency of *d* in the original population?

10. The rate of mutation of *agouti* to *nonagouti* in mice is 3×10^{-5} and the selection coefficient of the *nonagouti* allele is 0.2. What are the expected equilibrium allele frequencies?

11. Dwarfism in humans results from an autosomal dominant allele; it has been estimated that the frequency of mutation, *normal* → *dwarf* is 4.5×10^{-5}, and that the fitness of the *dwarf* allele is 0.25. What is the expected equilibrium frequency of the *dwarf* allele?

12. If $s = 0.8$ and $q = 0.4$, what are the expected frequencies of genotypes B_1B_1, B_1B_2, and B_2B_2?

13. Warfarin kills rats by interfering with their blood clotting; unfortunately, rats develop resistance as a consequence of mutation: sensitive → resistant. In the presence of warfarin, the fitnesses are 0.68, 1.00, and 0.37 for *ss*, *rs*, and *rr* respectively. Calculate the expected equilibrium frequencies after long-term use of warfarin.

14. The frequency of individuals affected by a rare autosomal dominant allele is 4×10^{-6}. If 70 percent of individuals with this allele die before breeding, estimate the mutation rate from normal to mutant.

15. In a population, genotypes are distributed as follows:

AA	Aa	aa
0.984064	0.015872	0.000064

If the mutation rate $A \rightarrow a = 5 \times 10^{-6}$, and the reverse rate is 0, calculate the selection coefficient of *a*.

16. If $q = 0.01$, and homozygous recessive individuals die *in utero*, what is the expected allele frequency after one generation? After two generations?

Chapter 15

Master Problems

The problems that appear in this chapter are meant to challenge you. Most problems require the use of many concepts presented throughout the text. Work the problems step by step, going from simple to complex. The first seven problems deal with classical genetics, and the remainder with bacterial genetics or molecular biology. Answers are presented in the answer section, but detailed solutions are not presented. Instead, hints and references to the appropriate chapters are given.

1. Two recessive genes in *Drosophila,* vermillion *(v)* and brown *(br),* affect eye color. Flies mutant for both traits are white. A true-breeding vermillion female is mated to a true-breeding brown male. The F_1s are then selfed to produce the F_2. For each case predict the expected F_2 phenotypic ratios.
    a. Assume vermillion is X-linked and brown is autosomal.
    b. Assume both are autosomal and unlinked.
    c. Assume both are autosomal and linked by 20 map units.
    d. Assume both are autosomal and linked by 60 map units.

2. White (X^w) is an X-linked recessive gene; cinnabar *(cn)* and sepia *(se)* are independent autosomal recessive traits in *Drosophila*. Females who are homozygous and males who are hemizygous for white have white eyes, regardless of what other alleles are present. In addition, individuals who are homozygous for both cinnabar and sepia are also white. The following crosses were made; then the F_1s were allowed to mate among themselves to produce F_2s.

Cross	Parents
1	white female × sepia male
2	sepia female × cinnabar male
3	cinnabar female × white male
4	white female × white male

The following vials of F_2 progeny were obtained. Match the cross with the correct vial.

		vial		
A	B	C		D
		females	males	
9 red	4 white	9 red	17 white	3 cinnabar
3 cinnabar	3 red	3 cinnabar	9 red	1 white
3 sepia	1 sepia	3 sepia	3 cinnabar	
1 white		1 white	3 sepia	

3. Mexican hairless dogs have very little hair. When hairless dogs are crossed, ⅔ of the progeny are hairless and ⅓ have straight hair. When the hairless progeny interbreed, they produce the same result as the original hairless dogs. When the straight progeny interbreed, all the progeny are straight. Suppose one of the hairless progeny mates with a true-breeding wire-haired, and produces equal numbers of hairless and wire-haired. Predict the phenotypic frequencies from a cross of:
   a. wire-haired × wire-haired
   b. wire-haired × straight

4. The ancient biped *Anser alchemister* was used by royalty for years because it was capable of producing golden eggs when fed diets of different metals. A breeding program was undertaken and a number of mutants were isolated. A recessive gene *hg* resulted in the formation of mercury-coated eggs, and the birds suffered from chronic mercury diarrhea. A second recessive gene *sn* resulted in tin-plated eggs, and the birds suffered from lacerated oviducts. Finally, a dominant gene *Fe* caused rust-coated eggs that were attracted to any nearby magnet. *Fe* was lethal in the homozygous condition; such embryos aborted before being coated. The various mutants blocked the pathway as indicated below.

$$sn \qquad\qquad hg \qquad\qquad Fe$$
$$\text{lead} \longrightarrow \text{tin} ---|\longrightarrow \text{mercury} ---|\longrightarrow \text{iron} ---|\longrightarrow \text{gold}$$

   Two individuals, each heterozygous for all three genes, are mated.
   a. What fraction of the live progeny will be gold?
   b. What fraction of the live progeny will be tin?
   (problem 4 courtesy of K. Singer)

5. Four *Drosophila* mutants are named jaunty wings *(j)*, fat body *(ft)*, balloon wings *(ba)* and clot eyes *(cl)*. Using the data derived from the following crosses, derive a suitable genetic map.

   Cross A:
   true-breeding jaunty fat female × true-breeding balloon, clot male
   ↓

   F₁   all wild-type

   Cross B:
   F₁ male from cross A × jaunty fat balloon clot female
   ↓
   253 jaunty fat males
   245 jaunty fat females
   243 balloon clot males
   259 balloon clot females

   Cross C:
   F₁ female from cross A × jaunty fat balloon clot male
   ↓

jaunty fat	160
balloon clot	162
jaunty fat balloon	158
clot	165
fat clot	8
jaunty	7
fat balloon clot	9
jaunty balloon	9

fat	77
fat balloon	78
jaunty clot	75
jaunty balloon clot	80
jaunty fat clot	2
wild-type	4
balloon	3
jaunty fat balloon clot	3
TOTAL	1000

(courtesy of R. MacIntyre)

6. The following is a map of part of the X chromosome of *Drosophila:*

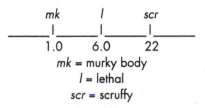

mk = murky body
l = lethal
scr = scruffy

The mutant allele l is maintained in females heterozygous for a specially marked X chromosome that contains the dominant mutation Bar *(B)* and inversions which cover the entire chromosome. In these females, one of the X chromosomes contains the mutant *B* allele and the inversions; all other genes on this chromosome are wild-type. The other X chromosome has the normal gene arrangement, as well as wild-type alleles except for *l*. Such a female was crossed to a murky, scruffy male, and the non-Bar females were kept. These females were crossed to wild-type males and the progeny scored. List the expected frequencies; assume the coefficient of coincidence in this region is 0.5.

7. Deaf mutism was observed in two families in Ireland with the following pedigrees.

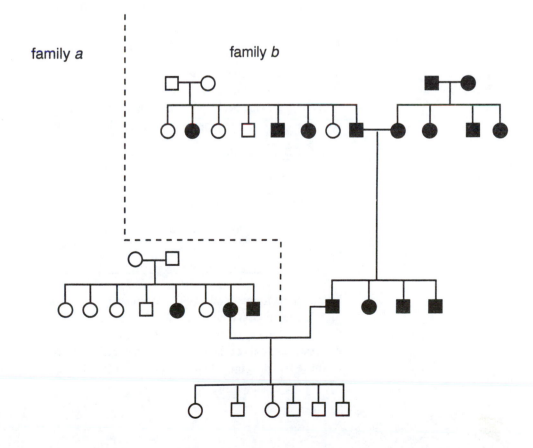

family *a*

family *b*

a. Indicate the probable mode of inheritance of this trait in family *a*.

b. Do the same for family *b*.

c. Are the factors determining deaf mutism in the two families the result of one or more genes? Explain.

8. A bacterial strain *lys⁺ his⁺ val⁺* is used as a donor, and *lys⁻ his⁻ val⁻* is the recipient. Initial transformants are isolated on minimal medium containing *his* and *val*.

a. What are the genotypes that will grow on this medium?

b. These colonies are replicated to *min + his*, and 75 percent of the original colonies grow. What are the genotypes that will grow on this medium?

c. The colonies are also replicated to *min + val*, and six percent of the colonies grow. What genotypes will grow on this medium?

d. Finally, the original colonies are replicated to minimal. No colonies grow. From this information, what is the genotype that grows on *min + his*? on *min + val*?

e. Based on the above information, which gene is closer to *lys*?

f. The original transformation is repeated but the original plating is on *min + lys + his*. Fifty colonies appear. These colonies are replicated to determine their genotypes and the following results appear.

val⁺ his⁺ lys⁺	0
val⁺ his⁻ lys⁺	37
val⁺ his⁺ lys⁻	3

Based on all the results, what is the most likely gene order?

9. Which of the following *E. coli* strains can hydrolyze lactose and under what conditions?

a. $i^+p^+o^+z^+/i^+p^+o^-z^+$

b. $i^-p^-o^+z^+/i^+p^+o^+z^-$

c. $i^+p^+o^+z^+/i^+p^-o^-z^+$

d. $i^+p^+o^+z^+/i^+p^+o^-z^-$

e. $i^-p^+o^+z^+/i^+p^-o^-z^-$

f. $i^+p^+o^+z^-/i^+p^-o^-z^-$

10. You are working with an exotic organism and have discovered an inducible operon for the production of silk *(sk)*. You have discovered that it is composed of four regions in the following sequence:

$$Q\ R\ S\ T$$

but the location of the operator and promoter have not been identified. The gene for the repressor is found to be located far from the operon. It is known that two different genes are necessary for the production of silk. Various deletions of the operon are isolated and mapped; their locations appear below (//// = deleted areas).

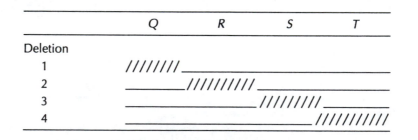

Deletion 1 is found to make silk continuously; deletions 2, 3, 4 never make silk.

a. Which region(s) could represent the operator?

b. Which region(s) could represent the promoter?

c. Partial diploids of the following genotypes are constructed and their ability to make silk determined (– = never make silk; C = constitutive; I = inducible).

Genotype	Silk Production
$Q^+ R^- S^+ T^+/Q^- R^+ S^+ T^+$	C
$Q^+ R^+ S^+ T^-/Q^+ R^+ S^- T^+$	–
$Q^+ R^+ S^- T^+/Q^+ R^- S^+ T^+$	I

Based on this additional information, which region contains the promoter?

11. Listed below are the enzyme activities of four mutants, *e, r, u,* and *y,* that affect ß-galactosidase in *E. coli*. One mutant is in the *z* gene, one is in the operator, one is in the promoter, and one is in the *i* gene. Determine which mutant is in which region. IPTG is used as an inducer of the *lac* operon.

Strain	Enzyme activity	
	-IPTG	+ IPTG
wild-type	1	1000
mutant *e*	0	0
mutant *r*	0	0
mutant *u*	1000	1000
mutant *y*	1000	1000
F´ *lacz+*/wild-type	2	2000
/e	1	1000
/r	1	1000
/u	1000	2000
/y	2	2000
F´ *lacz-*/wild-type	1	1000
/e	0	0
/r	0	0
/u	1000	1000
/y	1	1000

12. The following deletion strains are crossed (+ = wild-type recombinants recovered). Draw a map of the mutants. Do not be shackled by conventional maps.

	1	2	3	4	5
1	–	–	+	+	–
2		–	–	+	+
3			–	–	+
4				–	–
5					–

13. RII mutants of T4 phage will grow and produce large plaques on strain B; rII mutants will not grow on K12, a lambda lysogen. The following crosses are performed in strain B. The progeny of the crosses are diluted 10^{-7} and used to reinfect strain B. The following number of plaques are obtained:

1 × 2	250
1 × 3	250
2 × 3	250

The progeny of the above crosses are also diluted 10^{-4} and plated on K12. The following number of plaques are seen:

1 × 2	50
1 × 3	25
2 × 3	75

Draw a map of these three mutants and indicate distances between them.

14. Given below is the base sequence near the 3′ end of human ß-globin RNA and the amino acid sequence near the C-terminal end of the normal protein and three mutants, Olmstead, House, and Max.

5′ AAUGCCCUGGCCCACACUUAUCACUAAGCUAGCUUGACUAUGUG 3′

normal:	ala-leu-ala-his-thr-tyr-his-C
Olmstead:	ala-arg-ala-his-thr-tyr-his-C
House:	ala-leu-ala-his-thr-C
Max:	ala-leu-gly-pro-his-leu-ser-leu-ser-C

a. What is the stop codon used in normal hemoglobin?
b. Show the mutation that probably occurred in each mutant.

15. A DNA molecule is isolated and is shown to have the following base composition: 18% T, 32% A, 10% C, and 40% G.
a. What is the physical nature of this DNA?
b. You now perform a melting experiment and get the following result:

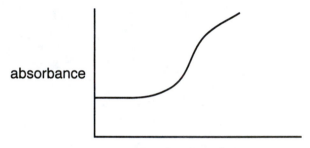

Why is this result unexpected?
c. Propose an explanation to account for this unexpected result.

Appendix A   Answers to Practice Problems

Chapter 1 Answers

1. **a.** The disease is recessive. If two individuals with the same phenotype produce offspring, some of whom have a different phenotype, both parents must be heterozygous. Since they are heterozygous, their phenotype must be dominant (concept 1-B).

   b. ¼. Let B = normal and b = blue diaper. The cross is $Bb \times Bb$. ¼ of progeny at each conception should be bb (concept 1-H).

2. $Yy \times yy$. We see two phenotypes in approximately a 1:1 ratio. We don't know which allele is dominant from this cross. The two phenotypes suggest one gene (concept 1-B), and the 1:1 ratio suggests a homozygote × a heterozygote (concept 1-D).

3. **a.** Short is dominant but homozygous lethal.

   b. ½ short : ½ normal.

   c. All normal. $ss \times ss$ (concept 1-A).

   We see two phenotypes in a 2:1 ratio. Since both flies have the same phenotype, short must be dominant (concept 1-E). The short parent must be heterozygous and the normal parent must be homozygous recessive. Therefore $Ss \times ss$ yields ½ Ss : ½ ss (concept 1-D).

4. Black is dominant, brown is recessive, and both parents were heterozygous. The progeny are in an approximate 3:1 ratio and both parents had the same phenotype (concept 1-C). Therefore, the simplest cross is $Bb \times Bb$.

5. All AB; or ½ AB, ½ A; or ½ AB, ½ B; or ¼ A : ¼ AB : ¼ B : ¼ O. Crosses can be AA × BB, AA × BO, AO × BB, or AO × BO. Different genotypes give the same phenotype, a result indicative of multiple alleles (concept 1-G).

   $$I^A I^A \times I^B I^B \text{ yields all } I^A I^B \text{ (AB)}$$
   $$I^A I^O \times I^B I^B \text{ yields } \tfrac{1}{2}\, I^A I^B \text{ (AB); } \tfrac{1}{2}\, I^B I^O \text{ (B)}$$
   $$I^A I^A \times I^B I^O \text{ yields } \tfrac{1}{2}\, I^A I^B \text{ (AB); } \tfrac{1}{2}\, I^A I^O \text{ (A)}$$
   $$I^A I^O \times I^B I^O \text{ yields } \tfrac{1}{4}\, I^A I^B \text{ (AB)}$$
   $$\tfrac{1}{4}\, I^A I^O \text{ (A)}$$
   $$\tfrac{1}{4}\, I^B I^O \text{ (B)}$$
   $$\tfrac{1}{4}\, I^O I^O \text{ (O)}$$

6. $Ll \times Ll$. Let L = long tail and l = no tail. We see three phenotypes in an approximate 1:2:1 ratio. One of the phenotypes (short) is intermediate between long ears and no ears. Therefore, we have incomplete dominance (concept 1-E).

7. Red is dominant and the cross is between two heterozygotes. We see two phenotypes in an approximate 3:1 ratio. Both parents have the same phenotype (concept 1-C).

8. white-1, white-2 : *Ww;* white-3 : *WW;* black-1 : *ww*

Since we see two different phenotypes in the progeny from white-1 × white-2, the whites must be heterozygous *(Ww)*, and black must be homozygous recessive *(ww)* (concepts 1-B and 1-C). The observed ratio is not 3:1, but remember that each offspring has a ¼ chance of being black (concept 1-H). Since white-1 × white-3 yields all white, white-3 must be homozygous *(WW)* (concept 1-A). The third cross suggests a testcross because of the 1:1 ratio (concept 1-D), but this result could have been deduced from information already given.

9. ⅙. The first cross is *se⁺se* × *se⁺se*. The red progeny will be either *se⁺se⁺* or *se⁺se;* ⅔ of them are expected to be *se⁺se* (concepts 1-C and 1-E). In order for the backcross to yield sepia, both parents must be heterozygous. If both are heterozygous, then ¼ of the progeny should be sepia (concept 1-C). Therefore, ⅔ (heterozygous) × ¼ = 2/12 = ⅙.

10. a. chestnut: C^cC^c; palamino: C^cC^w; cremello: C^wC^w

b. Mate chestnuts with cremellos.

We see three phenotypes coming from individuals with the same phenotype, and the ratio of the phenotypes approaches 1:2:1, suggesting incomplete dominance (concept 1-E). If we let C = gene for color, C^c = chestnut and C^w = cremello, C^cC^w must be palamino. The cross is then C^cC^w × C^cC^w to yield ¼ C^cC^c : ½ C^cC^w : ¼ C^wC^w. Crossing a palamino with either homozygote will give one-half palaminos (concept 1-D). Therefore, to get all palaminos, cross chestnuts (C^cC^c) with cremellos (C^wC^w).

11. gray: Cc^h; chinchilla: $c^{ch}c^{ch}$; light gray: $c^{ch}c^h$ or $c^{ch}c$; albino: cc. Before beginning, translate the information given into possible genotypes and phenotypes:

gray: CC, Cc^{ch}, Cc^h, Cc
chinchilla: $c^{ch}c^{ch}$
light gray: $c^{ch}c^h, c^{ch}c$
Himalayan: c^hc^h, c^hc
albino: cc

In order to get Himalayans in the third cross, one of the parents must contribute a c^h, and it must be the gray parent. Therefore the gray parent is Cc^h. Chinchilla must be $c^{ch}c^{ch}$, so the first cross must be Cc^h × $c^{ch}c^{ch}$, which yields ½ Cc^{ch} (gray) : ½ $c^{ch}c^h$ (light gray) (concepts 1-D and 1-G). For the second cross, try one of the genotypes for light gray, $c^{ch}c$. The cross is then Cc^h × $c^{ch}c$, which yields ¼ Cc^{ch} (gray) : ¼ Cc (gray) : ¼ $c^{ch}c^h$ (light gray) : ¼ c^hc (Himalayan). The other possibility for light gray, $c^{ch}c^h$, yields the same phenotypic ratios, but in this case the Himalayan progeny are c^hc^h.

12. a. blond: bb
light brown: bb^{mb}
medium brown: $b^{mb}b^{mb}$ or Bb
dark brown: Bb^{mb}
black: BB

The first two crosses suggest that blond and black result from homozygosity. Let these genotypes be *bb* and *BB* (for blond and black respectively). The third and fourth crosses give multiple results, but results that are single gene ratios. These results together suggest that we are dealing with multiple alleles, and that we have at least a third allele. Notice that some crosses of medium brown × medium brown yield all medium brown. This result suggests that medium brown could also be homozygous; call this genotype $b^{mb}b^{mb}$.

Now look at the third cross. We have assumed that blond is homozygous and that medium brown may be. If the cross is $bb \times b^{mb}b^{mb}$, then all progeny are bb^{mb}. In order to get light brown, we must have incomplete dominance between medium brown and blond. Now look at the second possible results for this cross. One-half of the progeny are blond. We know that blond must be homozygous, and for one-half of progeny to be blond, each parent must contribute one *b* allele; therefore the medium brown person in this case must be heterozygous for *b*. We know that the genotype cannot be bb^{mb}, for we already assumed this was light brown. We proposed three alleles: *B*, *b*, and b^{mb}. We must now use the third allele for the medium brown heterozygote. Therefore medium brown could be *Bb* or $b^{mb}b^{mb}$.

Only one other genotype remains, the genotype for dark brown. This must result from incomplete dominance between black and medium brown. Therefore dark brown is Bb^{mb}.

Because we see multiple ratios from the same phenotypes, we must be dealing with multiple alleles (concept 1-G). We also see some intermediate phenotypes that are inherited in a peck order type of dominance (concept 1-F).

b. ¼ light brown
¼ dark brown
½ medium brown

Using the genotypes from part (a) we get:

$$Bb^{mb} \times bb^{mb}$$
to yield
¼ bb^{mb} (light brown)
¼ Bb (medium brown)
¼ $b^{mb}b^{mb}$ (medium brown)
¼ Bb^{mb} (dark brown)

c. ½ medium brown : ½ dark brown

$$bb^{mb} \times BB$$
½ Bb (medium brown)
½ Bb^{mb} (dark brown)

13. Light green results from incomplete dominance between the dark green allele and some other allele; this second allele is lethal in the homozygous state. The first cross suggests a heterozygote × homozygote (concept 1-D). Since light green is the most frequent class in the second cross, assume it results from a heterozygote. This result suggests incomplete dominance (concepts 1-B, 1-C, and 1-E). The progeny in the second cross approach a 2:1 ratio, suggesting a lethal (concept 1-F). The light green allele must be lethal in the homozygous state. Let G^DG^D = dark green and G^DG^L = light green. The second cross can be drawn as:

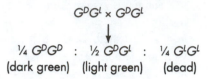

$$G^DG^L \times G^DG^L$$

¼ G^DG^D :   ½ G^DG^L :   ¼ G^LG^L
(dark green)   (light green)   (dead)

14. a. Yes.

   b. No.

Individuals with type A blood can be either I^AI^A or I^AI^O. If both are I^AI^O, ¼ will be expected to be I^OI^O or type O (concepts 1-B, 1-D, and 1-G).

15. red-1: C^AC^B; red-2: C^AC^C; red-3: C^AC^A; white: C^CC^C; pink: C^BC^C. The genotype C^BC^B is lethal. Look first at crosses 1 and 3; individuals with identical phenotypes yield different progeny. We therefore suspect multiple alleles (concept 1-G). Crosses 4 and 5 indicate that red is dominant over pink and white, and that red-3 must be homozygous (concept 1-A). Assume we have three alleles C^A, C^B, C^C. Let C^A = red. Red-1 and red-2 both must be heterozygous, but for different alleles. Let C^AC^B = red-1 and C^AC^C = red-2. The ratios from crosses with pink suggest that pink must also be heterozygous (concepts 1-C, 1-D, and 1-E). White must be homozygous (concept 1-D). Let C^CC^C = white. Therefore, C^BC^C = pink. In cross 1, the 2:1 ratio suggests a lethal (concept 1-F), but what genotype is lethal?

Diagram the cross:

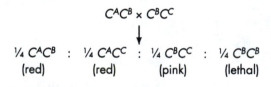

$$C^AC^B \times C^BC^C$$

¼ C^AC^B :   ¼ C^AC^C :   ¼ C^BC^C :   ¼ C^BC^B
(red)   (red)   (pink)   (lethal)

Using $C^AC^C \times C^BC^C$ in cross 3 yields the observed ratio. Thus we have three alleles, C^A, C^B, and C^C; C^BC^B is lethal; C^BC^C = pink, and C^CC^C = white.

Chapter 2 Answers

1. Red and long are dominant.

    $rr\,Ll \times rr\,Ll$
    $Rr\,Ll \times Rr\,ll$
    $R\text{-}\,ll \times RR\,Ll$
    $Rr\,Ll \times Rr\,Ll$
    $Rr\,ll \times rr\,Ll$

    Let R = red, r = brown, L = long, l = vestigial.

    Look first at those crosses that yield only two phenotypes; such crosses indicate that one gene is homozygous. Crosses 1 and 3 are such crosses. In cross 1 we see only brown eyes and in 3 we see only red eyes. The eye color must be homozygous in at least one parent. From these two crosses we can't determine whether red or brown is dominant. In cross 1 both parents have long wings, and we see a 3:1 ratio in the progeny. Long must be dominant and this cross must be $Ll \times Ll$. Similar logic applies to cross 3 (concept 2-B).

    In cross 2 we see an approximate 3:3:1:1 ratio, suggesting that the same gene is heterozygous in each parent. We see a 3:1 red : brown ratio. Therefore red is dominant and heterozygous in each parent: $Rr \times Rr$. We have already determined that long is dominant, which indicates the cross is $Rr\,Ll \times Rr\,ll$. Thus a 3:3:1:1 ratio indicates this general situation: $Aa\,Bb \times Aa\,bb$ (concept 2-D).

    In cross 4 we see four phenotypes in an approximate 9:3:3:1 ratio. This result indicates a mating between two double heterozygotes $Rr\,Ll \times Rr\,Ll$ (concept 2-C). In cross 5, we see a ratio of 1:1:1:1, suggesting a double testcross (concept 2-E). Since we have determined that red and long are dominant, these phenotypes must be heterozygous. Brown and vestigial are homozygous recessive.

2. $dydy\;unc^+unc \times dy^+dy\;uncunc$. Let dy = dumpy, dy^+ = long, unc = uncoordinated, unc^+ = coordinated. We see four phenotypes, so we probably have two genes (concept 2-A). Four classes appear in equal numbers, suggesting that one gene is heterozygous in each parent and that the other gene is homozygous. We can't tell which allele is dominant, but the 1:1:1:1 ratio suggests a double testcross (concept 2-E).

3. Purple is dominant to white, at least three genes are involved, and some type of gene interaction is present. The F_1 indicates that purple is dominant to all other colors. We see five phenotypes in the F_2; therefore we must have at least three genes. Recall that if we had only two genes and dominance, we expect only four phenotypes (concepts 2-A and 2-F). Normally with three genes we would expect eight phenotypes. We see only five phenotypes, so gene interaction must be involved (concept 2-J).

4. $7/16$. Two individuals with the same phenotype produce a new phenotype. This result suggests that we are dealing with two genes (concept 2-I), each of which can produce

a mutant phenotype. Hearing must be dominant to deafness, and the cross could be:

$$AA\ bb \times aa\ BB$$
$$\text{(deaf)}\quad\text{(deaf)}$$
$$\downarrow$$
$$\text{all } Aa\ Bb$$
$$\text{(hear)}$$

The cross is therefore *Aa Bb* × *Aa Bb*. This cross yields:

$9/16$ *A- B-* hear
$3/16$ *A- bb* deaf
$3/16$ *aa B-* deaf
$1/16$ *aa bb* deaf

Assign phenotypes to the genotypes to give 9 normal : 7 deaf, a modified 9:3:3:1 ratio (concept 2-J).

5. 5 hairy : 1 hairless. First diagram the cross: *Hh Ss* × *Hh Ss*. Use the product rule (concept 2-G) and the branching method to predict various genotypes.

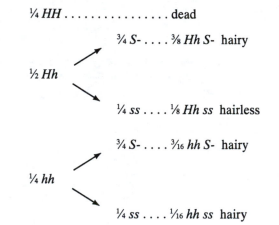

$1/4$ *HH* . . . . dead

$1/2$ *Hh*
   $3/4$ *S-* . . . . $3/8$ *Hh S-* hairy
   $1/4$ *ss* . . . . $1/8$ *Hh ss* hairless

$1/4$ *hh*
   $3/4$ *S-* . . . . $3/16$ *hh S-* hairy
   $1/4$ *ss* . . . . $1/16$ *hh ss* hairy

This gives a ratio of $10/16$ hairy : $2/16$ hairless. We count only the flies that we see, so we get a 5 hairy : 1 hairless. We used the product rule (concept 2-G), and then modified the results because we had a lethal (concept 2-H).

6. **a.** $9/64$

    b. $3/64$

    c. $3/64$

    Let *A/a* = normal/albino, *B/b* = brown/blue, *D/d* = normal/diabetic, and *P/p* = normal/PKU. Diagram the cross:

    $$Aa\ Bb\ Dd\ Pp \times Aa\ bb\ dd\ Pp$$

    Multiply the individual probabilities (concept 2-G).

    a. $3/4$ normal × $1/2$ brown × $1/2$ normal × $3/4$ normal = $9/64$

    b. $3/4$ normal × $1/2$ blue × $1/2$ galactosemic × $1/4$ PKU = $3/64$

    c. $1/4$ albino × $1/2$ blue × $1/2$ galactosemic × $3/4$ normal = $3/64$

7. **a.** 3 dom : 1 rec.

    b. 1 dom : 1 mutant *b* : 2 mutant *a*

Both F_1 ratios are derivatives of a 9:3:3:1 ratio (concept 2-J). To get a 15:1 ratio at least one dominant allele must be present in the progeny; *A- B*, *A- bb*, and *aa B-* all show the dominant phenotype. The cross in question then becomes *Aa Bb* × *aa bb*, a double testcross, so we expect a ratio of 1:1:1:1 (concept 2-E). Therefore we get:

¼ *A- B-* normal
¼ *A- bb* normal
¼ *aa B-* normal
¼ *aa bb* mutant

To get a 9:4:3 ratio in cross *b*, one mutant allele masks the effect of the other gene as follows:

9 *A- B-* normal
3 *A- bb* mutant *b*
3 *aa B-* mutant *a*
1 *aa bb* mutant *a*   (concept 2-J)

The cross in question is again a double testcross, *Aa Bb* × *aa bb*, which produces:

¼ *A- B-* normal
¼ *A- bb* mutant *b*
¼ *aa B-* mutant *a*
¼ *aa bb* mutant *a*   (concept 2-E)

8. **a.** $\frac{9}{32}$

   b. 0

   c. $\frac{9}{32}$

   d. 0

   e. ⅛

For each part use the product rule (concept 2-G).

a. ¾ *A-* × ½ *B-* × 1 *C-* × ¾ *D-* = $\frac{9}{32}$

b. Inspection will show that all individuals must be *Cc*, and there is no chance of *cc*.

c. ¾ *A-* × ½ *bb* × *C-* × ¾ *D-* = $\frac{9}{32}$

d. Again all individuals are expected to be *Cc*, so none can be *cc*.

e. ½ *Aa* × ½ *Bb* × 1 *Cc* × ½ *Dd* = ⅛

9. Dark is dominant and heterozygous in both dogs; either long or short is dominant and heterozygous; the other individual is homozygous recessive. The ratio is almost exactly 3:3:1:1, suggesting a cross of the following form: *Aa Bb* × *Aa bb* (concepts 2-A and 2-D). Dark must be dominant since ¾ of progeny are dark. We can't tell whether long or short is dominant. The cross could be either *Dd Ll* × *Dd ll* or *Dd ss* × *Dd Ss*.

10. **a.** ⅛

    b. ⅜

Since polydactyly is rare, it is reasonable to assume any affected individual will be heterozygous. Both must be heterozygous for curling, since their fathers were normal, homozygous recessive. Let P/p = polydactyly/normal and C/c = curling/non-curling. The cross can then be drawn as: $Pp\ Cc \times pp\ Cc$ and we use the product rule (concept 2-G).

a. ½ normal × ¼ straight = ⅛

b. ½ polydactylic × ¾ curling = ⅜

11. a. purple: *AA BB CC*
    white-1: *aa BB CC*
    white-2: *aa bb CC*
    white-3: *aa bb cc*

b. 1 purple : 1 red : 2 white.

c. 4 white : 1 red : 1 brown : 1 blue : 1 purple.

Since all of the F_1 are purple, purple must be dominant. We see five phenotypes in cross 3, therefore we must have at least three genes (concept 2-F) and the white-3 parent must be homozygous for all three recessive genes.

There is a lot to do before we can answer the questions. We must first determine the mode of inheritance of each eye color. Look first at the cross with white-1. The F_2 appear in an approximate 3:1 ratio, suggesting that only one gene is heterozygous in the F_1. Let the A gene be recessive in white-1. Therefore white-1 is *aa BB CC* (concept 2-K).

Now look at white-2. We see three phenotypes in a 9:4:3 ratio, suggesting that white-2 is homozygous for two recessive alleles (concept 2-J). Let *aa bb CC* = white-2. Cross 2 can then be diagrammed as:

$$AA\ BB\ CC \times aa\ bb\ CC$$
$$\downarrow$$
$$Aa\ Bb\ CC$$
$$(\text{purple})$$
$$\downarrow$$
$$\text{selfed}$$
$$\downarrow$$

9 *A- B- CC* purple
3 *A- bb CC* red
3 *aa B- CC* white
1 *aa bb CC* white
(concepts 2-C and 2-J)

The F_1 in cross 3 must be heterozygous for all three genes. Use the branching method and the product of probabilities rule (concept 2-G) to calculate expected frequencies.

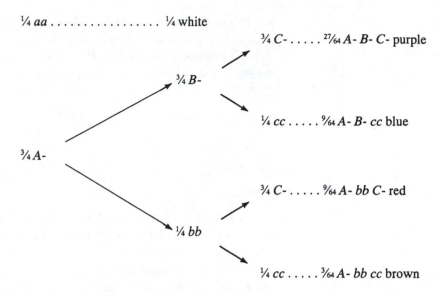

¼ *aa* . . . . ¼ white

¾ *C*- . . . . . ²⁷⁄₆₄ *A- B- C-* purple

¾ *B*-

¼ *cc* . . . . . ⁹⁄₆₄ *A- B- cc* blue

¾ *A*-

¾ *C*- . . . . . ⁹⁄₆₄ *A- bb C-* red

¼ *bb*

¼ *cc* . . . . . ³⁄₆₄ *A- bb cc* brown

There are 128 progeny and the observed ratios are almost exactly the predicted ratios.

The F₁ from cross 2 is *Aa Bb CC*, and the testcross is *Aa Bb CC × aa bb cc*. We recognize this as a double testcross and expect:

¼ *Aa Bb CC* purple
¼ *Aa bb CC* red
¼ *aa Bb CC* white
¼ *aa bb CC* white
(concept 2-E)

The F₁ from cross 3 is *Aa Bb Cc*, so the testcross is *Aa Bb Cc × aa bb cc*, a triple testcross, and we expect eight equally frequent classes:

⅛ *Aa Bb Cc* purple   ⅛ *Aa bb CC* red
⅛ *Aa bb cc* brown   ⅛ *Aa Bb cc* blue

The remaining four classes all have *aa* and are therefore white.

12. a. *AA BB* × *aa bb;* any *A* produces white, as does *aa bb*.

  b. All white; 3 white : 1 red.

The F₁ progeny suggest a cross involving at least one homozygote, but if this were so, we wouldn't expect anything but white in the F₂ generation. So we must propose that two genes are involved. If we divide both numbers by eight, we get a 13:3 ratio, which is a modified 9:3:3:1 ratio (concept 2-J). The white F₁s must be heterozygous for two different genes, *Aa Bb*. A mating between two such heterozygotes produces:

9 *A- B-* white
3 *A- bb* white
3 *aa B-* red
1 *aa bb* white

The two white parents must be *AA BB* and *aa bb*.

If the first parent is crossed to the F₁, *AA BB* × *Aa Bb*, we get all *A- B-*, white. If the second parent is used, resulting in the cross *aa bb* × *Aa Bb*, we get ¼ *Aa Bb* (white), ¼ *Aa bb* (white), ¼ *aa Bb* (red), ¼ *aa bb* (white) or 3 white : 1 red.

13. line 1: *aa BB cc.*

line 2: *AA BB cc.*

line 3: *AA bb cc.*

line 4: *aa bb cc.*

We see five phenotypes in cross 4, so all three genes must be heterozygous (concept 2-F). Therefore, albino 4 must be *aa bb cc*. In cross 2, we get a result from a single heterozygous gene (i.e., 3:1). Since all albinos must be *cc*, only this locus is heterozygous in the F₁s; therefore, albino 2 is *AA BB cc*. Crosses 1 and 3 yield progeny in approximately a 9:4:3 ratio, indicating two heterozygous genes, and a modified 9:3:3:1 ratio (concept 2-J). Let *A* and *C* be heterozygous in cross 1, and *B* and *C* in cross 3. Therefore, 1 = *aa BB cc* and 3 = *AA bb cc*.

Cross 1 yields:	Cross 3 yields:
9 *A- B- C-* gray	9 *A- B- C-* gray
3 *aa B- C-* cinnamon	3 *A- bb C-* black
3 *A- B- cc* albino	3 *A- B- cc* albino
1 *aa B- cc* albino	1 *A- bb cc* albino

The only remaining phenotype to account for is chocolate; it must be *aa bb C-*. We looked at ratios and went from simple to complex (concept 2-K).

14. Scarlet and brown are recessive and interact to produce white. The ratio is almost 9:3:3:1, so we have a double heterozygote in the F₁s (concepts 2-A, 2-B, and 2-C). Let *s⁺* = wild, *s* = scarlet; *br⁺* = wild; *br* = brown. The cross is then:

$$s^+s^+ \; brbr \times ss \; br^+br^+$$
$$\downarrow$$
all *s⁺s br⁺br*
$$\downarrow \text{ self}$$
9 *s⁺- br⁺-* red
3 *s⁺- brbr* brown
3 *ss br⁺-* scarlet
1 *ss brbr* white

15. golden female: *Gg Bb.*
golden male: *Gg bb.*
black male: *gg Bb.*

The ratios indicate two genes (concept 2-B) that yield a modified 3:3:1:1 ratio (concepts 2-D and 2-J), suggesting gene interaction. Group the colors first into golden vs. non-golden. In cross 1, we see a 3:1 ratio, indicating that the golden gene is heterozygous in each dog. Let *G-* = golden and *gg* = non-golden. Black and brown appear in a ratio of 1:1, indicating a heterozygote × homozygous recessive (concept 2-B), but we can't tell which allele is dominant from cross 1. In cross 2, we see a 3:1 black : brown ratio, indicating black is dominant and that each individual is heterozygous for this gene. Let *B* = black and *bb* = brown. The golden female must be heterozygous for both genes, *Gg Bb*. The golden male must be *Gg bb*. The black male must be *gg*, or else it would be golden; therefore, it is *gg Bb*.

16. 12 red : 4 scarlet : 3 prune : 1 white. Set up the cross *Aa Bb Cc* × *Aa Bb Cc* and use the branching method to calculate probabilities (concept 2-G); then assign phenotypes to genotypes (concept 2-H).

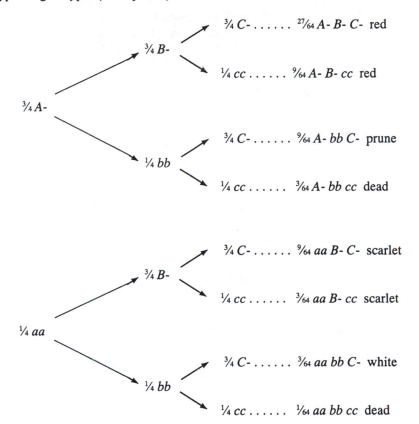

Chapter 3 Answers

1. **a.** 39 pairs.

   b. 39

   It has two copies of each, and 2 × 39 = 78. Meiosis halves the number of chromosomes, and ½ × 78 = 39 (concept 3-A).

2. **a.** 64. Since $n=6$, $2^6 = 64$ (concept 3-B).

   b. ¹⁄₆₄

   The chance of a gamete getting A is ½. Similarly, the chance of B, C, D, E, or F is also ½. The chance of all occurring together is the product of the individual chances:

   $$\tfrac{1}{2} \times \tfrac{1}{2} \times \tfrac{1}{2} \times \tfrac{1}{2} \times \tfrac{1}{2} \times \tfrac{1}{2} = \tfrac{1}{64}$$

3. About 8 million. Twenty-three pairs means $n=23$, and $2^{23} = 8 \times 10^6$ (concept 3-B).

4. **a.** $2c$.

   b. $2c$.

   c. $4c$.

   Cells at the end of meiosis I have half the number of chromosomes, but each chromosome is doubled. Since the DNA of an egg (after meiosis II) comes from the separation of chromatids, cells at the end of meiosis I must have a $2c$ amount of DNA. A cell following mitosis has 23 pairs of single chromosomes. If one set of single chromosomes = c, then two sets = $2c$. The chromosomes have duplicated before the onset of meiosis; therefore, $2 \times 2c = 4c$ (concept 3-D).

5. **f.** Homologous chromosomes will pair during meiosis. Each gamete gets one of each chromosome, A, B, C, and D (concept 3-A). Fertilization fuses two cells with the above chromosomal complement. Since root cells are somatic tissue, they will be diploid.

6. **a.** ⅛

   b. ⅛

   c. ⅜

   The number of chromosomal combinations is 2^n, where n = number of different chromosomes (concept 3-B). Thus there are 2^3, or eight possible combinations. The chance of getting one member of a pair is ½; therefore the chance of getting all three from one parent is $(½)^3 = ⅛$. The possible combinations with two maternal chromosomes and one paternal are $P'Q'R$, $P'Q R'$, and $P Q'R'$ (concept 3-A). Since there are eight different combinations, the fraction is ⅜.

7. A gamete from wheat will have 21 chromosomes, and a gamete from corn will have ten chromosomes. Even if the 10 corn chromosomes could pair with 10 wheat chromosomes, a highly unlikely event, the remaining 11 wheat chromosomes could not pair, and would randomly segregate during meiosis. Each gamete would get an

incomplete set, and most gametes would not survive. If fertilization did occur, the zygotes would have extra chromosomes (trisomic) or would be missing some chromosomes (monosomic or nullosomic) (concept 3-C).

8. **a.** 7

   b. 14

   c. 21

   In the tube nucleus, one of the pollen nuclei results from meiosis, and is therefore haploid (concept 3-A). A leaf cell is diploid. The endosperm results from the fertilization by a haploid pollen nucleus of a diploid nucleus, yielding a triploid cell.

9. **a.** 240

   b. 120

   c. 60

   The primary spermatocyte is diploid and will undergo meiosis to yield four cells; therefore, $4 \times 60 = 240$. The secondary spermatocyte has completed one meiotic division, and has one more division to go: $2 \times 60 = 120$. The spermatid is haploid and will mature into a sperm (concept 3-A).

10. **a.** 60

    b. 60

    The primary oocyte is diploid and will undergo meiosis, but only one functional ovum results from each primary oocyte (concept 3-A). The secondary oocyte will divide to produce an ovum and a polar body.

11. 256. The number of combinations is 2^n, where n = the number of different chromosomes in the set (concept 3-B).

Chapter 4 Answers

1. The wife probably has not been unfaithful. Since the woman's father was hemophilic, he must have given his X chromosome to her (concept 4-B). Since she is normal, she is therefore heterozygous. In order for a male to be hemophilic, he must have only one hemophilic allele. One such allele could come from the mother.

2. Cross straight females with frizzled males. For the sexes to be different, the female must be homozygous. If she is heterozygous, ½ of males will be frizzled and ½ will be straight (concept 4-D). The female can't be homozygous for the dominant trait. If this were true, both sons and daughters would receive the X-bearing dominant chromosome, and thus show frizzled. If the female is homozygous recessive (straight) and the male is frizzled, all sons get the straight chromosome and all daughters receive the frizzled chromosome (concept 4-E).

3. Long is dominant to short and autosomal; red is dominant to brown and X-linked. Let $+$ = long, s = short, X^R = red. X^r = brown.

$$ss; X^R X^R \quad \times \quad ++; X^r Y.$$

We first look at the F_1 and see that red and long must be dominant. We see four phenotypes in the F_2s, indicating that we have two genes involved. But only two of the four phenotypes appear in the females, suggesting X-linkage for one of the genes (concept 4-C).

Consider the female parent. If wing length were X-linked, all the F_1 males should have short wings. This is not observed; therefore, the gene for wing length must be autosomal.

We now look at eye color. The F_1 female must be heterozygous for all genes. One-half of F_2 males should get a normal X chromosome and ½ should get the mutant chromosome (concept 4-D). We see 47 brown eyes and 53 red eyes, suggesting that eye color is X-linked. Wing length in both males and females is approximately a 3:1 ratio, what we expect for an autosomal gene. The 3:3:1:1 ratio in males suggests one autosomal and one X-linked gene (concept 4-F).

4. **a.** Short bristles is X-linked dominant, but is a recessive lethal. We see a difference in both the phenotypes and the numbers of males and females, suggesting an X-linked gene that is hemizygous lethal (we see no short bristled males) (concepts 4-C and 4-G). Since we see two phenotypes in the females, short must be dominant, and the cross is:

$$X^S X^s \times X^s Y.$$

   b. All long progeny of both sexes. In order to have a long female, she must be homozygous. The cross is:

$$X^s X^s \times X^s Y.$$

5. The female is heterozygous for the X-linked alleles for color. We see different phenotypes in males and females, indicating X-linkage (concept 4-C). The female

must be heterozygous and X-inactivation must be occurring (concept 4-H). Let X^b = black and X^o = orange. The cross is then:

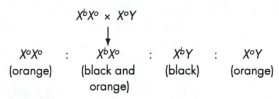

6. Color is sex-linked, and the male is the homogametic sex. We see a difference between males and females, indicating some type of sex-linkage (concept 4-C). Since all members of a given sex are identical, we are not dealing with heterozygous parents (concept 4-D and note). Setting up the cross in the typical way:

$$X^GX^G \times X^gY$$

predicts X^GX^g females and X^GY males. In this case both the males and the females should be green, a prediction inconsistent with the observations. Therefore, our initial cross must be in error; we assumed that the female is the homogametic sex.

Assume that the male is the homogametic sex. The cross is then:

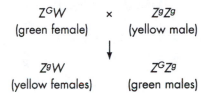

7. Color is sex-linked, green is dominant, and males carry two alleles for color. It is only the third cross that alerts us to sex-linkage, as we see a difference between males and females (concepts 4-A, 4-B, and 4-C). The second cross indicates that green is dominant to yellow. Recall that in birds, the male is the homogametic sex *(ZZ)*. If we let G/g = green/yellow, the crosses can be diagrammed as follows:

$$Z^gZ^g \times Z^gW \qquad Z^GZ^G \times Z^gW \qquad\qquad Z^gZ^g \times Z^GW$$

$$\downarrow \qquad\qquad\qquad \downarrow \qquad\qquad\qquad\qquad \downarrow$$

$$Z^gZ^g \; Z^gW \qquad Z^GZ^g \; Z^GW \qquad\qquad Z^GZ^g \; Z^gW$$

(all yellow)   (all green)   (green male) (yellow female)

8. F_1: all gray females; all yellow males. F_2: ½ gray, ½ yellow of both sexes. We see a difference in the phenotypes of the sexes in the F_2, suggesting some type of sex-linkage (concept 4-C). The F_1s indicate that gray is dominant to yellow. The F_1 females from the cross must be heterozygous, and the two phenotypes in the F_2 males result from each of the X chromosomes in the F_1 female. Let X^+ = gray and X^y = yellow. The cross is:

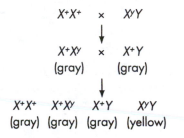

The cross in question is then:

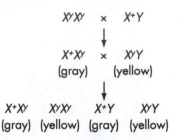

9. **a.** Scaly skin is probably an X-linked dominant.

   b. ½

   We see a difference in male and female children, suggesting some type of sex-linkage (concept 4-C). Scaly skin cannot be Y-linked, or all sons would have been affected (concept 4-B). Since all of the daughters and none of the sons have scaly skin, scaly skin must be X-linked dominant (concept 4-E). If S/s = scaly/normal, the original mating is $X^sX^s \times X^sY$. All daughters from this mating must be heterozygous. One-half of all children will be expected to receive the X^s chromosome (concept 4-D).

10. **a.** wild females, yellow males.

    b. 3 wild : 3 yellow : 1 vestigial : 1 vestigial, yellow in both sexes.

    c. 3 wild females : 1 vestigial female; 3 wild : 3 yellow : 1 vestigial : 1 vestigial, yellow male.

    Let X^+ = red, X^y = yellow, vg^+ = long, vg = vestigial

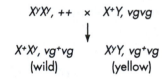

(concept 4-B)

Use the branching method for the F_2.

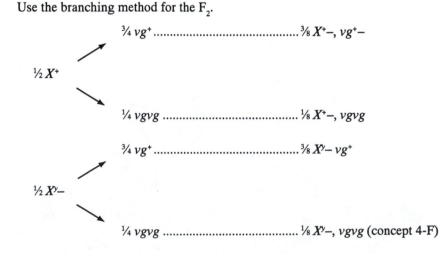

For the reciprocal cross,

$$X^+X^+, vgvg \times XY, vg^+vg^+$$

$$\downarrow$$

$$X^+XY, vg^+vg \times X^+Y, vg^+vg$$

All F_2 females will get X^+ from the male and the autosomal gene will give a 3:1 ratio. The males will be as in the above example (concepts 4-E and 4-F).

11. The female parent carries an autosomal gene for orange, and the male parent carries an X-linked gene for orange. Since the F_1s are wild (red), we must have two different genes involved (see chapter 2), and the orange genes must be recessive. We see a difference in the sexes of the F_2, so we must be dealing with some type of sex-linkage (concept 4-C). If both genes were X-linked, we should have seen orange F_1 males. We don't, so we have one autosomal and one X-linked gene. The female must carry the autosomal gene. If she carries the X-linked gene, the F_1 males should be orange. The male must carry the X-linked gene. One autosomal and one X-linked gene will produce a 3:3:1:1 ratio in at least the F_2 males (concept 4-F). We see 5 orange : 3 red among the F_2 males, a modified 3:3:1:1 ratio (see chapter 2). Let a = the X-linked orange, and b = autosomal orange. The crosses are then:

$$bb, X^+X^+ \quad \times \quad ++, X^aY$$

$$\downarrow$$

$$+b, X^+X^a \quad \times \quad +b, X^+Y$$
$$F_1 \text{ (red)} \qquad \text{(red)}$$

F_2 Females		Males	
3 X^+-, $+-$	red	3 X^+-, $+-$	red
1 X^+-, bb	orange	3 X^a-, $+-$	orange
		1 X^+-, bb	orange
		1 X^a-, bb	orange

12. **a.** $X^{N\,+}X^{+v}, ++; X^{++}Y, ee.$

b. normal F_1: 3 normal, red, tan : 3 normal, vermillion, tan : 1 normal, red, ebony : 1 normal, vermillion, ebony in both sexes.

Notch F_1: females	males
3 notch, red, tan	3 normal, red, tan
3 normal, red, tan	1 normal, red, ebony
1 notch, red, ebony	
1 normal, red, ebony	

We see no notched males, so notch must be lethal in the hemizygous state (concept 4-G). Since the males have vermillion eyes, the female parent must be heterozygous for vermillion (concepts 4-C and 4-D). If X^N = notch,

X^v = vermillion, X^+ = normal, and $+/e$ = tan/ebony, we can diagram the cross:

$$X^{N+}X^{+v}, ++ \quad \times \quad X^{++}Y, ee$$

$$\downarrow$$

$X^{N+}X^{++}$, +e	$X^{++}X^{+v}$, +e	$X^{N+}Y$, +e	$X^{+v}Y$, +e
(tan, notched)	(tan)	(dead)	(vermillion, tan)

Now set up the F$_2$s:

$$X^{++}X^{+v}, +e \quad \times \quad X^{+v}Y, +e$$

$$\downarrow$$

3 $X^{++}-$, +−	normal, red, tan
1 $X^{++}-$, ee	normal, red, ebony
3 $X^{+v}-$, +−	normal, vermillion, tan
1 $X^{+v}-$, ee	normal, vermillion, ebony

The cross to the notched female is $X^{N+}X^{++}$, $+e \times X^{+v}Y$, $+e$. One-half of the males will get X^{N+}, and will die (concepts 4-D and 4-G); those that survive will have normal wings and red eyes. Among the males, ¾ will be tan (see chapter 1). The females will be:

3 $X^{N+}X^{+v}$, +−	notch, red, tan
1 $X^{N+}X^{+v}$, ee	notch, red, ebony
3 $X^{++}-$, +−	normal, red, tan
1 $X^{++}-$, ee	normal, red, ebony

13. There are two genes involved, one autosomal recessive that produces brown eyes, and one X-linked recessive that produces white eyes. Any fly homozygous/hemizygous for white will be white, regardless of what other genes are present. The fact that the F$_1$s are wild-type suggests two different genes (see chapter 2), and the different F$_2$ results for males and females suggests at least one X-linked gene (concept 4-C). One-half of the F$_2$ males are white, a ratio expected for an X-linked recessive gene (concept 4-D). We see a 3:1 red : brown ratio, expected for an autosomal gene. The F$_2$ females show a 3:1 ratio for red to brown, suggesting that all females have at least one normal X chromosome. Let $X^+\!-\!A- $ = red, $X^+\!-\!aa$ = brown, X^w = white. The cross is then:

$$X^+X^+ \, aa \quad \times \quad X^wY \, AA$$

$$\downarrow$$

$X^+X^w \, Aa$	$X^+Y \, Aa$
(all red)	

$$\downarrow$$

$$\text{self}$$

3 X^+-, $A-$ red	3 $X^+Y \, a-$ red
1 X^+-, aa brown	1 $X^+Y \, aa$ brown
	3 $X^wY \, A-$ white
	1 $X^wY \, aa$ white

We see a modified 3:3:1:1 ratio in the F$_2$ males, indicating one autosomal and one X-linked gene (concept 4-F, see chapter 2). The observed numbers are close to a 4:3:1 ratio.

14. **a.** 3: *AA, BB,* and *AB.*

    b. only one, either *A* or *B.*

The *Drosophila* female will make both forms of the subunits in all cells, and these can combine to form *AA, BB,* and *AB.* In humans, only one of the two X chromosomes is active (concept 4-H), so a given cell will make either *AA* or *BB.* It is likely that both forms will be present, but only one form will appear in any given cell.

Chapter 5 Answers

1. **a.** linked.

   b. *WS/ws.*

   c. 10.7 m.u.

   We recognize the cross as a testcross and see two different frequencies of classes. The genes must be linked (concepts 5-A and 5-D). The most frequent classes are unspotted, short (*W–S–*) and spotted, long (*ww ss*). Therefore the female is *WS/ws* (concept 5-B). To calculate RF, recombinants/total × 100 = $^{17}/_{158}$ × 100 = 10.7 m.u. (concept 5-A).

2. **a.** linked.

   b. repulsion (*trans*).

   c. 28.6%.

   The cross is a testcross. If the genes were not linked, we would expect a 1:1:1:1 ratio (concepts 5-A and 5-D). The alleles that are in *cis* will appear in the majority classes, and the majority classes are tall, smooth and short, rough. Therefore, tall and rough are in *tans*. If we let *T/t* = tall/short and *R/r* = rough/smooth, the cross is then *Tr/tR* × *tr/tr*. Recombinants are *TR* and *tr;* RF = (105 + 110)/751 × 100 = 28.6%.

3. c__6__a__3__b__4__f__8__d____10__e

   Start with the greatest distance first, *a-e* = 25. Since *a-f* = 7, we try *f* between *a* and *e*:

   $$a\_\_7\_\_f\_\_\_\_18\_\_\_\_e.$$

   Gene *d* can be on either side of *f: afde* or *adfe.* Since *f-d* = 8 and *d-e* = 10, the order must be *afde.* Therefore:

   $$a\_\_7\_f\_8\_d\_10\_e.$$

   Since *b-d* = 12 and *a–b* = 3, we get:

   $$a\_3\_b\_\_4\_\_f\_\_8\_\_d\_\_10\_\_e.$$

   If *c-f* = 13, *c* must be six to the left of *a*, confirming the observed *c-b* of nine. We generated overlapping maps and added distances (concept 5-L).

4. Gene *d* is in the middle. Group reciprocal classes together (concept 5-E).

DeF	76
dEf	82
def	30
DEF	24
Def	15
dEF	18
deF	4
DEf	1

   The parent must be *DeF/dEf* (concept 5-B) and classes *DEf* and *deF* represent double crossovers (concept 5-F). Compare non-recombinant classes with double crossovers.

Alleles *eF* and *Ef* are together in both cases. Therefore, *D* must be in the middle (concept 5-G). We can rewrite the heterozygous parent as *FDe/fdE*.

5. a. *dy_____35.5__b_____5.4_bt*

b. 0.74

The F_1 tell us that all three mutant alleles are recessive. Let +/*dy* = slim/dumpy, +/*b* = white/black, +/*bt* = straight/bent. The testcross is:

$$dy + +/+ b \ bt \times dy \ b \ bt/dy \ b \ bt$$

Group the reciprocal classes together (concept 5-E).

1.	+ *b bt*	301	non-recombinant
2.	*dy* + +	305	"
3.	+ + +	169	single *d-b*
4.	*dy b bt*	172	"
5.	+ *b* +	19	single *b-bt*
6.	*dy* + *bt*	21	"
7.	+ + *bt*	8	double crossover
8.	*dy b* +	6	"

Determine the DCO as + + *bt* and *dy b* + (concept 5-F). The bent and dumpy alleles are together in parents and in DCO. Therefore, black is in the middle (concept 5-G). You should draw the DCO to confirm this statement. With the gene order, we deduce that classes 3 and 4 represent single exchanges between *dy-b,* and classes 5 and 6 represent single exchanges between *b-bt*.

We calculate the *dy-b* distance as

$$(169 + 172 + 8 + 6)/1000 \times 100 = 35.5$$

We calculate the *b-bt* distance as

$$(21 + 19 + 6 + 8)/1000 \times 100 = 5.4 \text{ (concept 5-H)}.$$

Expected DCO = $(0.355) \times (0.054) = 0.019$

Observed DCO = $14/1000 = 0.014$

CC = observed/expected = $0.014/0.019 = 0.74$ (concept 5-H).

6. a. *k + cd/+ e +*

b. *k____7__e____5__cd*

The genes are linked (concept 5-A). The initial cross is:

$$k \ cd +/k \ cd + \times + + e/+ + e$$

and the F_1s are *k cd +/+ + e* in any order. The last two phenotypic classes are the least frequent, and thus the double crossover results. These two classes will allow us to determine the order. If the order is *k cd e,* a double crossover will yield *k + +* and + *cd e*. The order must be *k e c d* (concepts 5-F and 5-G). Therefore,

$$RF \ k\text{-}e = (32 + 34 + 2 + 1)/1000 \times 100 = 7$$

and

$$RF \ e\text{-}cd = (25 + 23 + 2 + 1)/1000 \times 100 = 5$$

We followed the procedure in concept 5-H.

7. The two genes are linked, but by more than 50 m.u. Use the symbols *dy* and *b* for dumpy and brown, respectively. The F₁ indicate that dumpy and brown are recessive; the F₁ must be *dy b/+ +*. The ratio is clearly not the expected 9:3:3:1 for independent genes, so we must have linkage (concept 5-A). Since there is no crossing over in *Drosophila* males, we can test for linkage for genes more than 50 m.u. apart. The expected ratio for such linkage is 5:1:1:1 (concept 5-K). We expect a ratio of 100:20:20:20. Our results are quite close to this ratio. You should run a chi-square to verify this last statement.

8. **a.** round and slimy are linked; spiked assorts independently.

   b. *RS/rs; Sp/sp.*

   c. 20.5 m.u.

   We see four majority classes in equal frequencies, suggesting that one gene is not linked (concept 5-J). If two genes are not linked, they should produce 1:1:1:1 ratio among the majority classes. Comparing round/flat with spiked/smooth or spiked/smooth with slimy/slimeless produces this 1:1:1:1 ratio. Therefore, round and slimy are linked. The non-recombinants will appear in the majority classes; round, slimy and flat, slimeless are these classes. The alleles are in *cis, RS/rs* (concepts 5-A and 5-B).

   $$RF = (38 + 33 + 40 + 35)/710 \times 100 = 20.5\%$$

9. Genes *A* and *B* are linked by 20 m.u.; *C* assorts independently. We don't see eight equal classes, so at least some form of linkage is involved (concept 5-A). If all three genes were linked, we would see only two majority classes instead of four. Therefore, only two of the genes are linked (concepts 5-B and 5-J). To determine which two genes are linked, look at only two genes at a time within the majority classes.

amiable, active	780
amiable, active	810
nasty, benign	820
nasty, benign	790

Since only two phenotypic classes make up the majority classes, *A/a* and *B/b* are linked. Confirm that *C* is unlinked by observing a 1:1:1:1 ratio for genes *A/a* and *C/c* (concept 5-J). Therefore, the cross can be diagrammed as:

$$Ab/Ab; cc \quad \times \quad aB/aB; CC$$
$$\downarrow$$
$$Ab/Ab; Cc$$

The testcross is:

$$Ab/Ab; Cc \quad \times \quad ab/ab; cc$$

Since the alleles are in repulsion in the F₁, the recombinants between the two genes will be *AB* and *ab*. We can then calculate RF as:

$$(192 + 208 + 195 + 205)/4000 \times 100 = 20 \text{ m.u.}$$

136 APPENDIX A

10. $Qr = qR = 42.5\%$; $QR = qr = 7.5\%$.

First set up the cross:

$$Qr/qR \times qr/qr$$

Recognize that classes Qr and qR will be the most frequent (concept 5-B). Since RF Q-R = 15, 15 percent of the progeny will be recombinants, QR and qr (concept 5-I). Reciprocal classes will be equal, so $QR = 7.5\% = qr$; $Qr = qR = 42.5\%$ (concept 5-E).

11.

+	b	stw	0.393
fz	+	+	0.393
+	+	+	0.072
fz	b	stw	0.072
+	b	+	0.032
fz	b	stw	0.032
+	+	stw	0.003
fz	b	+	0.003

Before beginning the math, determine the single exchanges between *fz-b* as + + + and *fz b stw* and the single exchanges between *b-stw* as + *b* + and *fz* + *stw*; DCOs are + + *stw* and *fz b* +. Since *fz–b* = 15 and *b–stw* = 7, the expected frequency of DCO is (0.15) (0.07) = 0.0105.

$$CC = observed\ DCO/expected\ DCO; 0.6 = observed/0.0105$$
$$observed = (0.6)(0.0105) = 0.006$$

Since reciprocal classes are equal, we expect 0.003 for each class, + + *stw* and *fz b* +.

The distance *fz–b* = 0.15 = (singles + doubles)/total = (singles + 0.006)/total; singles = 0.144, and each class equals 0.072.

The distance *b–stw* = 0.07 = (singles + 0.006)/total; singles = 0.064, and each class equals 0.032.

The non-recombinant classes represent the remaining progeny, 1.000 – 0.214 = 0.786, and each class equals 0.393 (concept 5-I).

12. *Ab,Cd; Ab,cD; aB,Cd; aB,cD*. Diagram the cross:

$$AB/AB;\ CD/CD \times ab/ab;\ cd/cd$$

$$AB/ab;\ CD/cd \times ab/ab;\ cd/cd$$

The least frequent classes will result from recombination between both sets of genes (concept 5-B). These classes will be *Ab Cd, Ab cD, aB Cd,* and *aB cD*.

Chapter 6 Answers

1. **a.** autosomal recessive.

   b. I-1, I-2, II-1, II-2, III-4, III-5

   c. ⅔

   d. ⅙

   Since the normal individuals have an affected child, the trait must be recessive (concept 6-B). It can't be X-linked recessive; I-1 would have to have the trait in order for II-3 to be affected. Any two normal individuals who have mutant children must be heterozygous (see chapter 1). Since II-3 must be *pp*, all normal children, III-4 and III-5, must be heterozygous. Since the cross of II-1 × II-2 is *Pp* × *Pp*, both III-2 and III-3 have ⅔ chance of being *Pp*. They are normal, so they can't be *pp*. Since III-3 has ⅔ chance of being *Pp*, and since III-4 is *PP*, the chance that both are *Pp* is ⅔ × 1 = ⅔ (concept 6-H). If two heterozygotes mate, there is ¼ chance of getting an affected child. Therefore, the total chance is ⅔ × ¼ = 2/12 = ⅙.

2. Y-linked, X-linked dominant, X-linked recessive, autosomal dominant. Y-linked traits are passed only from father to son. If the trait is dominant, at least one of the parents should have the trait. If the trait is X-linked recessive, all of the daughters should get a normal X from the father (concepts 6-B and 6-C).

3. A: X-linked recessive, autosomal recessive; B: X-linked dominant, autosomal dominant; C: Y-linked, autosomal dominant, autosomal recessive, X-linked recessive; D: autosomal dominant.

   In A, the trait is recessive, since it skips a generation (concept 6-B). If the woman is heterozygous, ½ of sons are expected to be affected (concept 6-C). If the trait is autosomal, we expect ¼ of progeny to be affected.

   In B, the trait must be dominant. If it were recessive, both parents would be homozygous, and all the progeny would be affected. If the trait is X-linked, all daughters will be affected (concept 6-E).

   In C, if the trait is Y-linked, only sons will show it. If it is autosomal dominant, the woman must be homozygous recessive, and her husband is probably heterozygous (concept 6-A). One-half of the progeny of such a mating (*Aa* × *aa*) should be affected. If it is autosomal recessive and the woman is a carrier, ¼ of the children should be affected. If it is X-linked recessive and the woman is a carrier, both daughters could have received the normal X chromosome and both sons the mutant one.

   In D, the trait must be dominant. If it were recessive, all progeny should be affected. It can't be X-linked dominant, for all daughters would be expected to show it (concept 6-E).

4. *A* on 6; *B* on 2; *C* on 13; *D* on 12; *E* on 10. Gene A is present in clones X, Y, and Z, and chromosome 6 is common to these three clones. B is present only in Y, and 2 is the only chromosome unique to Y. Similar logic allows the assignment of the other genes (concept 6-J).

5.

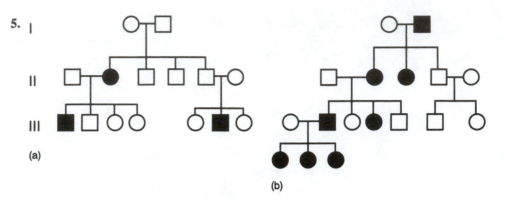

(a)

(b)

For a trait to be recessive, two normal individuals must have an affected child (concept 6-B). If a trait is X-linked recessive, a male with the allele should show the trait. Since the male in *Ia* does not show the trait, he cannot have an X-linked mutant allele. An X-linked dominant trait must appear in all daughters of an affected male (concept 6-E).

6. ⅛. Individuals in I must be $I^B I^O$ and $I^A I^O$ respectively to produce a child with type O blood. Now try to assign genotypes to other individuals. II-1 must be $I^O I^O$, II-2 must be $I^A I^O$, and II-5 must be $I^A I^B$. II-6 must be $I^B I^O$, or else all children would have been *AB* or *B*. III-2 must be $I^A I^O$. III-3 has a ½ chance of being homozygous for I^B and a ½ chance of being $I^B I^O$. If III-3 has the latter genotype, there is a ¼ chance of a child being $I^O I^O$. Therefore ½ × ¼ = ⅛ (concept 6-H).

7. a. X-linked dominant;

    b. autosomal dominant, X-linked dominant, Y-linked;

    c. X-linked recessive, Y-linked;

    d. X-linked dominant, Y-linked, autosomal dominant.

    We can only eliminate the modes that are completely contradicted by the pedigree. In (a), we eliminate X-linked dominant because daughters in II are normal (concept 6-E). Autosomal dominant is possible even though we see no affected daughters. Females I-1 and II-4 could be heterozygous, even though this possibility is unlikely (concepts 6-A and 6-G). In (b), we eliminate all dominant modes, since the trait skips a generation (concept 6-B). Y-linked traits are passed only from father to son (concept 6-F). In (c), we eliminate X-linked recessive, since all sons of II-5 should have the trait (concept 6-C). Females have the trait so it is not Y-linked. If I-1 and II-1 were heterozygous for an autosomal recessive, albeit unlikely, (concept 6-G), ½ of progeny should show the trait. In (d), we eliminate Y-linkage because females show it, and X-linked dominant because II-4 has normal daughters (concept 6-E). We eliminate autosomal dominant because two normal individuals produce affected children (concept 6-B).

8. a. ½

    b. ¼

    Individuals with dominant traits are usually heterozygous (concept 6-A), so the man is probably *Hh* and the son has a one-half chance of being *Hh*. His wife must be *hh*. If he is *Hh*, the cross is then *Hh* × *hh*, which yields a ½ chance of a child with Huntington's (see chapter 1). Therefore, the chance of their having a child with Huntington's is ½ × ½ = ¼ (concept 6-H).

9. **a.** $^{243}/_{1024}$

   b. $^{135}/_{512}$

   c. $^{9}/_{1024}$

   In (a), since all the children have the same phenotype, each child will have the same probability of having no molars. Therefore, $(^3/_4)^5 = {}^{243}/_{1024}$ (concept 6-G). In (b), $n = 5$, $s = 3$, $t = 2$, $p = ^3/_4$ and $q = ^1/_4$. Therefore, $P = 5!/3!\ 2!(^3/_4)^3\ (^1/_4)^2 = {}^{135}/_{512}$ (concept 6-J). When order is given, we multiply each probability, since the chance at each conception is constant. Therefore, $^3/_4 \times ^3/_4 \times ^1/_4 \times ^1/_4 \times ^1/_4 = {}^{9}/_{1024}$ (concept 6-G).

10. **a.** $^{27}/_{64}$

    b. $^{9}/_{4096}$

    With three children the formula becomes $3!/2!\ 1!\ (^3/_4)^2\ (^1/_4) = {}^{27}/_{64}$ (concept 6-J). The chance of:

    a normal boy or girl $= (^3/_4)\ (^1/_2) = ^3/_8$

    affected boy or girl $= (^1/_4)\ (^1/_2) = ^1/_8$

    We multiply these probabilities together to get $^3/_8 \times ^1/_8 \times ^1/_8 \times ^3/_8 = {}^{9}/_{4096}$ (concept 6-H).

11. $^1/_8$. Individual 2 must be heterozygous *Aa,* as must be *A*'s father. We assume *A*'s mother is *AA,* since there is no mention of the disease in his family. Therefore, *A* has $^1/_2$ chance of getting *a* from his father. If two heterozygotes mate, the chance of a recessive child is $^1/_4$, so $P = ^1/_4 \times ^1/_2 = ^1/_8$ (concepts 6-G and 6-H). Genetics knows no history; each child has an equal chance of having the disease.

12. **a.** $^3/_8$

    b. $^5/_{16}$

    Let T = taste and t = non-taste. The cross is therefore $Tt \times tt$, a testcross, so there is a $^1/_2$ chance of either taster or non-taster (see chapter 1). Therefore, $p = q = ^1/_2$, $n = 4$, $s = 2 = t$. $P = 4!/\ 2!\ 2!\ (^1/_2)^2\ (^1/_2)^2 = ^3/_8$ (concept 6-J).

    In (b), $n = 6$ and $s = t = 3$, so $P = 6!/3!\ 3!(^1/_2)^3\ (^1/_2)^3 = ^5/_{16}$. Note that as n increases, the P for the same ratio decreases because of additional possibilities.

13. **a.** $^1/_{32}$

    b. $^3/_4$

    Let M/m = absence/presence of molars, A/a = normal/albino, and T/t = normal/Tay-Sachs. The cross is then $mm\,Aa\,Tt \times Mm\,Aa\,Tt,$ which yields a $^1/_2$ chance of molars, $^3/_4$ chance of normal skin, and $^3/_4$ chance for normal with respect to Tay-Sachs. In (a) we multiply the probabilities: $(^1/_2)(^1/_4)(^1/_4) = ^1/_{32}$ (concept 6-H). In (b) there is a $^1/_2$ chance of no molars and a $^1/_4$ chance of Tay-Sachs. Since we are asking for either/or, not both, we add the probabilities: $^1/_2 + ^1/_4 = ^3/_4$ (concept 6-I).

14. **a.** Line B.

    b. Lines A and C.

We need to determine the lines that have chromosome 11; these lines are expected to be positive for the enzyme. We see that line B has chromosome 11 and that lines A and C have chromosome 5 (concept 6-K).

15. The trait is X-linked dominant and lethal in males. We see a difference in the phenotypes of the progeny, suggesting sex-linkage (concept 6-A, see chapter 4). We see no affected males, but we do see aborted males; these are probably males that received the dominant allele. The woman must be heterozygous for the trait. Let X^I = affected and X^i = normal. The cross is then:

$$X^I X^i \ \times \ X^i Y$$

$$\downarrow$$

$X^I X^i$	$X^i X^i$		$X^i Y$	$X^I Y$
(affected)	(normal)		(normal)	(dead)

Chapter 7 Answers

1. 34. Meiosis in *Q* and *R* produces gametes with seven and 10 chromosomes, respectively. The zygote has 17 chromosomes, and none of them can pair. For the hybrids to be fertile, each chromosome must duplicate itself. The hybrid has two sets from *Q* (2 × 7) and two sets from *R* (2 × 10). The hybrid is an allotetraploid (concept 7-H).

2. The son is probably $X^b X^b Y$. Begin by determining the genotype of the parents. Always assume they are normal unless evidence suggests otherwise. The woman must be $X^B X^b$ and the man must be $X^b Y$. If the son received the X^b from the mother and the Y from the father, he would be $X^b Y$, brown-toothed, but normal. The other phenotypes, especially poorly developed testes, suggest Klinefelter's syndrome, *XXY*. Nondisjunction probably occurred at meiosis I in the father to yield a sperm that is $X^b Y$ (concept 7-G). Alternatively, nondisjunction could have occurred at meiosis II in the mother to yield an egg with $X^b X^b$.

3. a. Only eight phenotypes are seen, and we expect $2^5 = 32$.

b. The F_1 female is probably heterozygous for an inversion that includes *c* and *d*.

c.

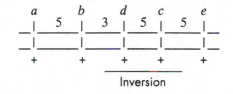

We suspect an inversion, since we see fewer than the expected number of phenotypes (concept 7-A). We can determine the location of the ends of the inversion by calculating RF between genes.

$$a–b = {}^{10}\!/_{200} \times 100 = 5 \text{ m.u., the given distance; no inversion}$$
$$b–c = {}^{6}\!/_{200} \times 100 = 3 \text{ m.u., less than expected}$$
$$d–e = {}^{10}\!/_{200} \times 100 = 5 \text{ m.u., less than expected}$$

We see no recombination between *c* and *d*; therefore *c* and *d* must be within the inversion. The distance from *b* to the breakpoint can be calculated from recombinants between *b* and *c-d*, or three m.u. The left end of the inversion is three m.u. to the right of *b*. Similar logic places the other end of the inversion five m.u. from *e* (concept 7-F). Therefore, the inverted chromosome of the original female is:

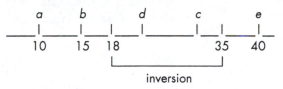

4. Band 1 = *q*, 2 = *p*, 3 = *r*, 4 = *u*, 5 = *t*, 6 = *s*. If a deletion allows the expression of a recessive allele, one of the bands spanned by the deletion must correspond to the gene in question (concept 7-B). Bands 1, 2, and 3 must correspond to genes *p*, *q*, and *r* in any order. Bands 2 and 3 are also missing in deletions B and D; phenotypes *p* and *r* are present in these strains.

Therefore, 1 = *q*. Compare deletions 2 and 3 which both span band 3. Gene *p* appears only in B; therefore, 2 = *p* and 3 = *r*. Deletions B and C both span band 4, and C and E span bands 4 and 5. Since *u* is the only trait common to all three deletions, $4 = u$. Similar logic places $t = 5$ and $s = 6$ (concept 7-D).

5. **a.** translocation.

   b. *Sh* is 19 m.u. from the breakpoint.

     Semi-sterility is often associated with translocations (concept 7-E). Since the *Sh* phenotype is also semi-sterile, the *Sh* parent must contain the translocation. The semi-sterile *sh* and the fertile *Sh* progeny result from recombination between the gene and the breakpoint. The RF gives the distance from *Sh* to the breakpoint (concept 7-F).

$$RF = (195 + 185)/2000 \times 100 = 19 \text{ m.u.}$$

6. **a.** Nine chromosomes; three sets of A, B, and C.

   b. sterile.

     Meiosis in a tetraploid will yield gametes with two sets of chromosomes (see chapter 3). Fertilization yields $2n + n = 3n$, or 3A, 3B, and 3C. Since the hybrid is triploid, it is likely to be sterile (concept 7-H, see chapter 3).

7. **a.** All females should be tan; deletion of part of the X chromosome from the male.

   b. 2 tan females : 1 yellow male.

     First diagram the cross by letting X^+ = tan and X^y = yellow:

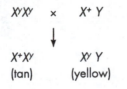

     The use of X rays alerts us to the possibility of chromosomal breaks. We see an unexpected recessive phenotype, suggesting a deletion of part of the X chromosome from the male (concept 7-B). The X chromosomes of the F_1 yellow female could be:

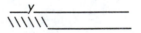

     If we cross this female to a tan, nonirradiated male, the cross becomes (X^* = deleted X chromosome):

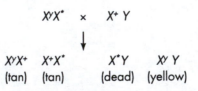

     The males that receive the deleted X chromosome die (concept 7-C).

8. 34. Meiosis in A and B will yield gametes with 11 and six chromosomes respectively. Fertilization will yield a hybrid with 17 chromosomes, none of which presumably can pair. If each chromosome in the hybrid doubles, a fertile polyploid will result (concept 7-H).

9. It is impossible to determine. Let X^C = normal vision and X^c = color-blind. The cross is then $X^C X^c \times X^c Y$. Turner's syndrome is XO. If nondisjunction occurred in the father, this would produce a sperm with XY and one with no sex chromosome. The daughter could get X^c from the mother. If nondisjunction occurred in the mother, the egg would have no X chromosome and would get X^c from the father (concept 7-G).

10. Nondisjunction occurs in meiosis II in a normal male. This problem requires that you follow sex chromosomes in a male through both divisions of meiosis. The two Y chromosomes must come from the male (concept 7-G, see chapter 3).

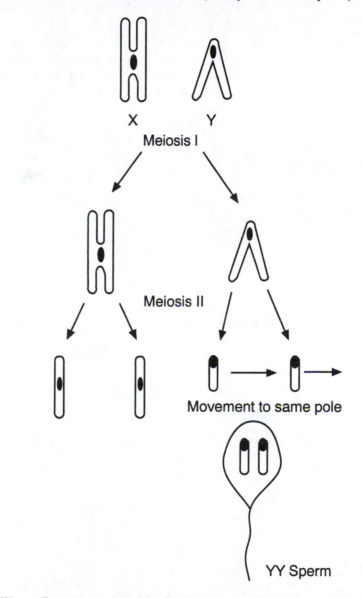

X   Y

Meiosis I

Meiosis II

Movement to same pole

YY Sperm

11. **a.** We see five percent recombination between *a* and *b*, and we expect 19 percent; therefore, there is possibly an inversion between *a* and *b*.

   b.

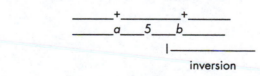

inversion

We see all the expected phenotypes, but the frequency of recombinants is much less than expected. A deletion would reduce map distance, but the given genotype and the frequencies of progeny suggest we do not have a deletion. The only other aberration that will reduce recombination is an inversion (concept 7-A). The RF *a-b* is $^{50}/_{1000} \times 100 = 5\%$. Therefore, *a* must be 5 m.u. from the beginning of the inversion that includes *b* (concept 7-F).

12. *c, d, a, b*. We see that inversions must have occurred to produce each new strain; we look for the simplest inversion to produce the new strain. Strain *d* could result from *c* by inverting 943 to yield 349. If 8734 in *d* is inverted, we arrive at the order in *a*. Finally, inverting 654 in *a* yields the order in *b* (concept 7-A).

13. Translocation from the tip of the X chromosome to the Y chromosome; cross the tan F_1 male to the yellow female and expect all tan males. Irradiation suggests a chromosomal break. Let X^+ = tan and X^y = yellow and diagram the cross.

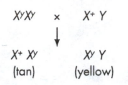

We expect all yellow males. The tan male must have received a normal allele for body color from the irradiated male. The most likely explanation is that a small piece of the X broke off and became attached to the Y:

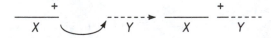

The X-Y translocation, because of +, will mask the *yellow* allele from the mother (concepts 7-F and 7-G). If this male is crossed to a yellow female, all the male progeny will receive the translocated Y, and will have tan bodies.

14. **a.** normal 15 and 21; normal 21, translocated 15; deficiency 21, translocated 15; deficiency 21, normal 15.

b. ⅓

It is best to draw the translocation and follow the 15 and 21 chromosomes through meiosis.

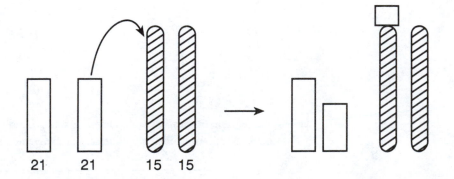

Meiosis will produce:

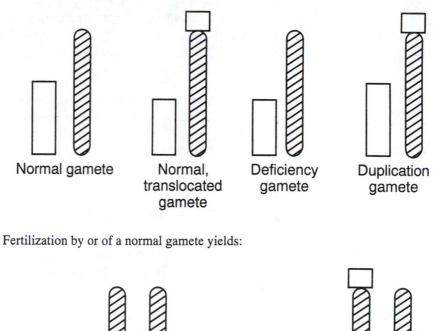

Fertilization by or of a normal gamete yields:

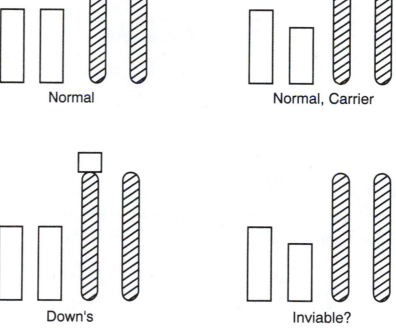

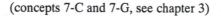

(concepts 7-C and 7-G, see chapter 3)

The situation is usually more complicated than drawn, and more than four gametes are often possible, depending on how much of the 21st chromosome is translocated. Refer to *familial Down's syndrome* and Robertsonian translocations in your text.

15. a. Notch is associated with a deletion; facet is located within the notch deletion.

   b.

notch deletion

Let X^N = notch, X^d = dwarf, and X^f = facet. Cross 1 tells us that the original notch female is heterozygous and that notch is dominant. The lack of notch males suggests that notch behaves as a recessive lethal (see chapter 4).

The first cross is therefore:

$$X^{N+}X^{++} \quad \times \quad X^{+d}Y$$

$$\downarrow$$

$$X^{N+}X^{+d} \quad X^{++}X^{+d} \qquad X^{N+}Y \quad X^{++}Y$$
$$\text{(notch)} \quad \text{(wild)} \qquad \text{(dead)} \quad \text{(wild)}$$

Cross 2 verifies that notch is lethal, as we again see no notch males. It also allows us to calculate RF between notch and dwarf. Draw the X chromosomes of the F_1 female:

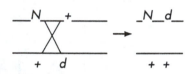

The wild-type males are recombinants and the distance is $^{34}/_{334} \times 100 = 10$ m.u. (see chapters 4 and 5). Therefore, notch is 10 m.u. from dwarf.

Cross 3 introduces the new gene, facet, that appears in some of the female progeny. If facet were dominant, all female progeny would be facet, and this is not seen. Facet must be recessive, and its appearance in some females suggests a deletion (concept 7-B). If notch is associated with a deletion, an X-linked deletion will be lethal when homozygous or in hemizygous males (concept 7-C). Assume facet lies within a deletion associated with notch. The dwarf, notch females result from recombination between notch and dwarf (see cross 2 explanation). This female is:

$$\frac{N \qquad d}{+ \qquad d}$$

We can diagram cross 3:

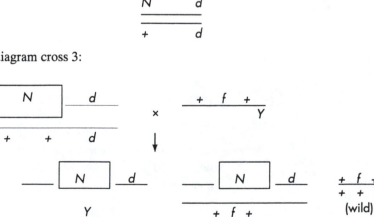

Cross 4 allows us to map facet and dwarf, and the RF can be calculated by examining male progeny in this cross. RF = $^{60}/_{500} \times 100 = 12$ m.u. Since notch is probably a deletion that ends 10 m.u. from dwarf, and since facet is within the deletion, the deletion must be at least 2 m.u. long (concept 7-F).

The best map is:

```
              f                    d
    ____|_____12_____|__
        | 2      |  10
   \\\\\\\\\\\\\|
     notch deletion
```

Chapter 8 Answers

1. a_____31____c____19.0___b

   Proceed as you would for any linkage analysis (see chapter 5). The most frequent classes, $+bc$ and $a++$, are non-recombinants, and the least frequent classes are double crossovers, $a+c$ and $+b+$. We can thus determine the gene order as $a\ c\ b$ (concept 8-A).

$$RF\ b\text{-}c = (34 +14 + 28)/400 \times 100 = 19.0\ \text{m.u.}$$
$$RF\ a\text{-}b = (52 +58 + 34 +28)/400 \times 100 = 43.5\ \text{m.u.}$$
$$RF\ a\text{-}c = (52 +14 + 58)/400 \times 100 = 31\ \text{m.u.}$$

2. 14 m.u. The cross is $nic^-\ thi^+ \times nic^+\ thi^-$. The only genotype that grows on minimal medium is $nic^+\ thi^+$, and this results from an exchange between the two genes. The other recombinant is $nic^-\ thi^-$; it will not grow on minimal. Thus the total recombinants $= 2 \times 35 = 70$, and $RF = {}^{70}/_{500} \times 100 = 14$ m.u.

3. a___10___●____8__c ●_____15.5_____b

   Analyze the first cross and classify each ascus as PD, NPD, and TT. Classes I and VI = PD, II and VII = NPD, and III, IV, and V = TT. Since PD = NPD, a and b are not linked (concepts 8-B and 8-C). Now classify each gene in each ascus as first or second division segregation (concept 8-E). This allows calculation of gene-to-centromere distances (concept 8-F).

$$a\text{-cent} = \tfrac{1}{2}(10 + 7 + 2 + 1)/100 \times 100 = 10\ \text{m.u.}$$
$$b\text{-cent} = \tfrac{1}{2}(10 + 18 + 2 + 1)/100 \times 100 = 15.5\ \text{m.u.}$$

   Proceed in a similar manner for the second cross. Since PD>>NPD, a and c are linked (concept 8-C).

$$c\text{-cent} = \tfrac{1}{2}(5 + 12 + 3)/100 \times 100 = 8\ \text{m.u.}$$

   Now calculate a-c distance as ($\tfrac{1}{2}$ TT + NPD)/total $\times$ 100 (concept 8-F).

$$a\text{-}c = \tfrac{1}{2}(5 + 8 + 12)/100 + {}^{3}/_{100} \times 100 = 15.5\ \text{m.u.}$$

   If a and c were on the same side of the centromere, a-c would be about 2 m.u. Since this result is not seen, a and c must be on opposite sides of the centromere.

4. 24. Gene-to-centromere distance $= \tfrac{1}{2}$ (second division segregation)/total $\times$ 100. Therefore the percent of second division segregation is $2 \times 12 = 24$ (concepts 8-E and 8-F).

5. a and c are linked by 5.5 m.u.; b and d are linked by 25 m.u. To determine the linkage, compare PD and NPD. In cases 1 and 3, PD = NPD; so a is not linked to b or d. In cross 4 PD>>NPD, so b and d are linked (concept 8-C). We calculate gene-to-gene distances as: [$\tfrac{1}{2}$(TT) + NPD]/total $\times$ 100 (concept 8-D).

$$a\text{-}c = [\tfrac{1}{2}(9) + 1]/100 \times 100 = 5.5\ \text{m.u.}$$
$$b\text{-}d = [\tfrac{1}{2}(30) + 10]/100 \times 100 = 25\ \text{m.u.}$$

6. 4. Since NPD result from a four-strand double crossover, we can assume NPD will be nonexistent due to the closeness of a and b (concept 8-C). Calculate gene-to-gene distance as $2 = [\tfrac{1}{2}(TT) + 0]/100 \times 100$; TT = 4 (concept 8-D).

7. ad____6.5___•_____12.5_____trp

First, classify asci for second division segregation: IV, V, and VI for *ad,* and III, V, VI, and VII for *trp* (concept 8-E). Gene-to-centromere distances are:

$$ad\text{-cent} = \tfrac{1}{2}(18 + 6 + 2)/200 \times 100 = 6.5 \text{ m.u.}$$
$$trp\text{-cent} = \tfrac{1}{2}(30 + 6 + 2 + 12)/200 \times 100 = 12.5 \text{ m.u.}$$

Now classify I and V as PD, II and VI as NPD, and III, IV, and VII as TT (concepts 8-B and 8-C). Since PD>>NPD, the genes are linked. To calculate:

$$RF = [\tfrac{1}{2}(30 + 18 + 12) + 8]/200 \times 100 = 19 \text{ m.u. (concept 8-D)}$$

8. •____23__x_6_y__7__z

You must analyze two genes at a time. Begin by classifying each ascus type.

Ascus	x-y	x-z	y-z
I	P	P	P
II	P	P	P
III	T	T	P
IV	P	T	T
V	T	T	P
VI	P	T	T
VII	P	T	T
VIII	P	T	T

We see no NPD, so all three genes are linked (concept 8-C). Calculate the gene-to-centromere distances (concept 8-F).

$$x\text{-cent} = \tfrac{1}{2}(70 + 4 + 4 + 2 + 6)/186 \times 100 = 23 \text{ m.u.}$$
$$y\text{-cent} = \tfrac{1}{2}(70 + 18 + 4 + 4 + 2 + 6)/186 \times 100 = 28 \text{ m.u.}$$
$$z\text{-cent} = \tfrac{1}{2}(70 + 18 + 14 + 4 + 4 + 6)/186 \times 100 = 31 \text{ m.u.}$$

Now calculate gene-to-gene distances (concept 8-D).

$$x\text{-}y = \tfrac{1}{2}(18 + 4)/186 \times 100 = 6 \text{ m.u.}$$
$$y\text{-}z = \tfrac{1}{2}(14 + 4 + 2 + 6)/186 \times 100 = 7 \text{ m.u.}$$
$$x\text{-}z = \tfrac{1}{2}(18 + 14 + 4 + 4 + 2 + 6)/186 \times 100 = 13 \text{ m.u.}$$

All three genes are on the same side of the centromere.

9. **a.** PD = 80, NPD = 4, TT = 16

   b. PD = 51, NPD = 7, and TT = 42

   We use the formula: distance = [NPD +½(TT)]/total × 100 (concept 8-D). For *(a)*, 12 = NPD + ½ (4NPD); NPD = 4. For (b), 28 = NPD + ½ (6NPD); NPD = 7.

10. 28 m.u. Again we use the relationship: distance = [NPD + ½ (TT)]/total × 100. Therefore, TT = PD = 12 NPD. Distance = 7NPD/25 NPD × 100 = 28 m.u.

Chapter 9 Answers

1. **a.** *ara nic gal* or *nic ara gal*.

   b. Select for *gal*, then score *gal⁺ ara⁺* and *gal⁺ nic⁺*.

   If the first order is correct, *gal⁺ ara⁺ <gal⁺ nic⁺*. Since *nic* and *ara* are co-transduced 40 percent of the time, they must be close and adjacent. If *gal* were in the middle, *nic⁺ gal⁺* would be more frequent than *nic⁺ ara⁺* (concept 9-A). If we select for *gal⁺*, and the order is *ara nic gal*, the genotype *gal⁺ ara⁺ nic⁻* requires two sets of exchanges, whereas *gal⁺ nic⁺* requires only one exchange. If the order is *nic ara gal*, *gal⁺ ara⁺* requires only one exchange, and should be more frequent than *gal⁺ nic⁺* (concept 9-C).

2. *a* and *b* are close; *c* is unlinked. We notice that *c⁺* and any other gene is quite rare, a situation indicating that *c* is far from *a* and *b*. Unlinked genes will not appear on the same piece of DNA; co-transformation will require two sets of exchanges (concept 9-B).

3.

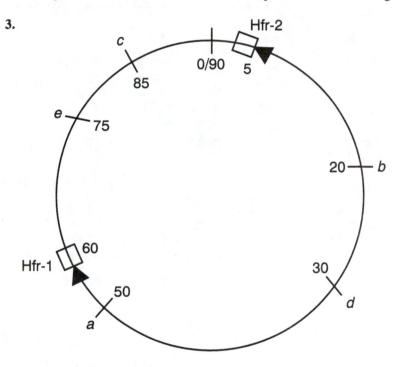

   In strain 1, order of transfer, as determined by time of first appearance, is *a d b c e*. For strain 2, the order is *b d a e c*. The bacterial chromosome is circular.

   First determine the time between genes:

   a-d = 20 minutes, *d-b* = 10 minutes, etc. Since the F factor is transferred last, and since *b* (at 20) appears 40 minutes after start, F factor is at 60 minutes, and *a* is 10 minutes from the F factor (at 50 minutes). Similar logic allows the placement of all other genes, and also the second F factor (concept 9-C).

4. Three genes. Gene *A:* mutants 1, 4, and 8; gene *B:* mutants 2 and 5; gene *C:* mutants 6 and 7. Mutant 3 probably contains a deletion that spans genes *A* and *C*. Begin by finding those mutants that do not complement. These should be in the same gene (concept 9-F). Mutants 2 and 5 are in the same gene. Initially, we suspect that 1, 3,

4, and 8 are in the same gene and different from the gene that contains 6 and 7. If mutant 3 is in gene *A*, it should complement 6 and 7, and it doesn't. One explanation is that 3 is a deletion spanning genes *A* and *C* (concept 9-G). Alternatively, mutant 3 could be in gene *A* but be a polar mutation (concept 9-J). Either of these two possibilities implies that the order is *B A C*.

5.

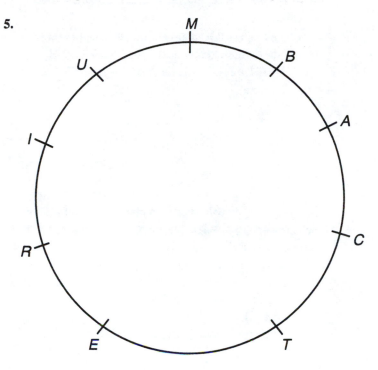

Arrange the orders so they overlap:

1.   *A C T E R*

2.   *T E R I U*

3.   *M B A C T*

4. *I U M B A*

Since the bacterial chromosome is circular, the order is as presented above (concept 9-C).

6. a. *rII-1* is probably a deletion and *rII-2* is a point mutant.

b. Revertants *revb* and *revc* probably contain second-site mutations.

The lack of revertants suggests a deletion, so *rII-1* is probably a deletion (concept 9-K). If no wild-type recombinants are recovered from the revertants, these revertants are probably suppressor or second-site mutations (concept 9-L).

7. *d e f*. We see that *f* and *d* are co-transduced the least. Therefore, *d* is probably far from *f*, and probably requires two sets of exchanges (concepts 9-A, 9-B, and 9-C). We see a higher co-transduction frequency for *e* and *f*, so *e* is closer to *f* than is *d*.

8. Mutation in *C*, mutation in promoter, or polar mutation in *E* or *D*. Since a mutation fails to complement with *C⁻*, it may be in the same gene (concept 9-F). If the mutant is *p⁻*, the diploid is *p⁻ E D C B A/p⁺ E D C⁻ B A*. The top DNA can never make RNA, and no complementation will occur (concept 9-J, see chapter 11). Another type of mutation that won't complement is a polar mutation in a gene before *C* (concept 9-J).

9. Strains 2, 5, and 7 are deletions.

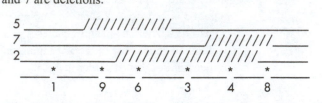

Plating on minimal medium allows the detection of revertants. Since deletions don't revert, they will not grow on minimal (concept 9-K). Having determined that 2, 5, and 7 are deletions, isolate these strains from the second set of data.

	2	5	7
A	–	–	–
B	–	–	+
C	–	+	–

Strain 2 gives no wild-type recombinants; therefore it must overlap the other two deletions (concept 9-H). Deletions 5 and 7 must not overlap. Mutant 2 gives the same results as strain A, so $A = 2$. Since B recombines with 7, B must be 5; so $C = 7$. Mutant 9 gives wild-type recombinants with deletions 2 and 7. It must be located in the region that is uniquely located in deletion 5 (concept 9-I). Similar logic places 8 in the region unique to 7, and 3 in the area unique to 2. Mutants 4 and 6 must lie within the deleted region common to 2 and 7, and 2 and 5, respectively. Mutant 1 gives wild-type recombinants with all deletions, and must be located outside all deleted areas. It could be located at either end of the map.

10. (a)

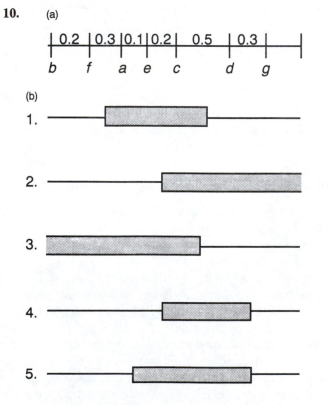

c. *a, b,* and *f* in *RIIA; e, c, d,* and *g* in *rIIB*

d. none.

Mutants *b* and *d* must be far apart, as must be *b* and *g; e* and *f* could be between *b* and *d:*

$$\underline{\quad\quad b\_0.2\_f\_0.4\_e\_\quad\_d\_0.3\_g}$$

Now try to place *a* and *c.* Since *a-b* = 0.5, *a* must be 0.3 to the right of *f.* Since *a-c* = 0.3, *c* must be to the right of *a,* or it would be at the same place as *f.* Mutant *c* must be to the right of *a,* and the distances are additive (concept 9-E). Look for minuses in the crosses; those mutants will be covered by the particular deletion. Deletion 1 must span mutants *a, c,* and *e,* since no wild-type recombinants appear (concept 9-I). Similarly, mutant 2 must span *c, d,* and *g.* Similar logic allows placement of deletions 3-5. Since *a* complements *e, a* must be in *rIIA,* as must be *b* and *f* (concept 9-F). All deletions are missing *c,* so none can give wild-type recombinants (concept 9-H).

11. *c a b pro.* We must set up the transduction, using two orders, and look for the order that will generate wild-type by a double exchange. This order will give a low number of wild-type transductants (concept 9-C). Assume the order is *b a pro.* The first crosses are then:

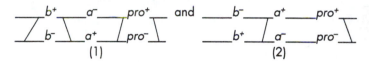

If this is the order, the first cross predicts wild-type< wild-type in the second cross, since two sets of exchanges are needed for the first cross. This result is not seen, so *b* must be closer to *pro* than *a.* Similar logic must be used to order *c* with respect to *a* and *b.*

12. 3%. We need to calculate total and recombinant progeny. Since all phage grow in strain *D,* the number growing here must be the total number of progeny, 200×10^7. The only thing that grows in strain *C* is wild-type, so these plaques must represent recombinants. However, the number obtained is only half the total number of recombinants; the double mutant will not grow. The number of recombinants is $2(30)(10^6) = 60 \times 10^6$.

$$RF = (60 \times 10^6)/(200 \times 10^7) \times 100 = 3\% \text{ (concept 9-E)}$$

Chapter 10 Answers

1. *GAA* to *GUA* or *GAG* to *GUG*. Looking at the code for *glu* and *val*, we see that a change of the *A* in the second position to a *U* will produce the new amino acid (concepts 10-A, 10-B, and 10-C).

2. These are the only possible single base changes of stop codons.

UAA can change to	*CAA gln UCA ser UAG stop*
	AAA lys UGA stop UAC tyr
	GAA glu UUA leu UAU tyr
UGA can change to	*CGA arg UAA stop UGG trp*
	GGA gly UCA ser UGC cys
	AGA arg UUA leu UGU cys
UAG can change to	*CAG gln UGG trp UAA stop*
	AAG lys UUG leu UAC tyr
	GAG glu UCG ser UAU tyr

   Note that if a new amino acid is *cys,* you know that the stop codon was *UGA* (concepts 10-A, 10-B, and 10-F).

3. **a.** mutation of *cys* codon to stop.

   b. mutation of *A* to *G* in *gln* codon.

   c. insertion of *U* in *leu* codon.

   GGX UUA AGA CAA UGC CAU AUU

   Only the third mutant allows you to determine the sequence of the bases in the normal RNA. Since many amino acids are changed, we should think immediately of a frameshift mutation (concept 10-D), beginning with the second amino acid. Mutant a is a truncated protein, so a premature stop must have been produced (concept 10-E). Mutant b shows one altered amino acid, so a missense is involved (concept 10-C). Write down the possible codons for the first three normal amino acids:

GGX	UUA	AGA
	G	G
	CUX	CGX

   and for the mutant:

GGX	UUC	AAA
	U	G

   If *leu* is *UUA/G*, an insertion of *U* will yield *UUU* for *phe*. The *leu* codon can't end in *G*, because no *lys* codons begin with *G*. Therefore, *leu* is *UUA*, and *arg* is *AGA/G*. The rest of the sequence can be determined by writing down all possible codons for each amino acid, and determining which one gives the desired sequence (concept 10-A).

4. **a.** alternating polymer of *ser* and *leu*. *UCUCUCUCUCUCUC* yields *UCU* and *CUC* codons.

   b. polymers of either *phe (UUC), ser (UCU)* and *leu (CUU)*.

   c. polymers of either *gln (CAA), asn (AAC)* and *thr (ACA)*.

d. polymers of *ile (AUA)* and *asn (AAU); UAA* is a stop signal.

e. polymers of *met (AUG)* and *asp (GAU); UGA* is stop signal.

We used the code to determine the amino acid that corresponds to a given codon (concepts 10-A and 10-B).

5. Three. Consider the sequence 5′ *AGACUC* 3′ in the middle of an RNA strand. The two codons are *AGA* and *CUC*. If the second *A* is changed to a *C*, the following sequence results: 5′ *AGCCUC* 3′. The mutant protein would be *ser-leu* instead of *arg-leu*. If the code is overlapping, the third base will appear in three codons: *AGA*, *GAC*, and *ACU*. The mutant RNA will be read as *AGC*, *GCC*, then *CCU* (concept 10-A).

6. **a.** *met-gln-cys-asn-pro-ala*

   b. *met-gln-ser-asn-pro-ala*

   c. *met-*

   d. *met-gln-leu-gln-ser-cys*

   e. *met-gln-cys-asn-pro-ala*

   We simply read the RNA in groups of three in a 5′ to 3′ direction. Mutant b yields only one amino acid change because we have a missense mutation (concept 10-C). Mutant c has produced a premature stop (concept 10-E). In mutant d, a *C* has been inserted into the third codon, causing changes in many codons and amino acids (concept 10-D). Note that mutant e has a point mutation in the RNA, but this mutant has a normal protein because of redundancy of the code.

7. *AGA*. First write down all possible codons: *AGA*, *AGG*, *CGX* (concept 10-A). Now write down possible codons for the mutants:

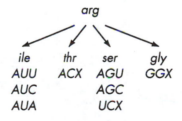

Now look for single base changes between the possible codons and the mutant codons (concept 10-B). *AGG* can't be the codon for *arg;* two bases would need to be changed to get *ile* codons. Similarly, two changes of *CGX* would be necessary to produce *thr* and *ile* codons. The only possible codon is *AGA* and all the codons are:

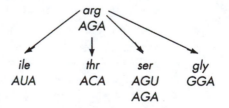

8. **a.** *gly, gly*

   b. 5′ *CGG* 3′ *(arg);* glycine may be inserted at some arginine codons.

Write down the mRNA that must be complementary to the anticodon, keeping in mind polarity:

normal tRNA: 3′ CCC 5′	mutant tRNA: 3′ GCC 5′
normal mRNA′ 5′ GGG 3′	mutant mRNA: 5′ CGG 3′
normal amino acid: *gly*	mutant amino acid: *arg*

The charging of an amino acid to a tRNA does not depend on the anticodon, so the altered tRNA will still carry *gly*. It will recognize an *arg* codon, and occasionally insert *gly* in place of *arg* (concept 10-G).

9. It is unlikely. Assume a mutagen causes a base to be inserted. All codons after the insertion will be altered, and many, if not all, amino acids will also be altered (concept 10-D). A chemical causing missense or point mutations will change only one base in one codon. Only one of the altered amino acids will be changed (concept 10-C), and it is unlikely that this one change will restore function to the protein.

10. No. Remember that mutations occur at the level of DNA, and that DNA is double-stranded. Write down the appropriate DNA sequence for each stop codon.

UAA: 3′ ATT 5′	UAG: 3′ ATC 5′	UGA: 3′ ACT 5′
5′ TAA 3′	5′ TAG 3′	5′ TGA 3′

There are no *C*s in the DNA for *UAA*, so hydroxylamine could not work here. If the *C* in the DNA for either *UAG* or *UGA* is changed to *T*, the resultant RNA has *UAA*, another stop codon (concepts 10-A and 10-B).

11. 5′ *AUG GCC UUU UCU CAC CGU GAG GUC CUC*...3′. Begin by writing all possible codons for each amino acid (concept 10-A). We notice that the altered sequence begins at position 26, so the insertion or deletion occurred at this codon (concept 10-D).

	25	26	27
Normal	*met*	*ala*	*phe*
	AUG	GCX	UUC/U
Mutant	*met*	*ser*	*leu*
	AUG	AGU/C	CUX
		UCX	UUA/G

A deletion of one base in the *ala* codon will not yield any *ser* codons. We also cannot make *UCX* by an insertion. If *ala* is *GCX*, the insertion of an *A* produces *AGCXUUC/U*. In order for amino acid 26 to be *leu* in the mutant, *leu* must be *CUX*. Therefore, the *ala* codon in the normal is *GCC*. Comparing amino acids 27, *phe* and *tyr*, *phe* must be *UUU* (concepts 10-A and 10-B). We see a truncated protein, so a stop must have been produced after codon 30 in the frameshift (concept 10-E), indicating that the third base in codon 30 must be *U*. Thus the codon for 30 is *CGU*. The partial revertant becomes normal once again at amino acid 32, indicating that the stop must have changed to a regular codon (concept 10-F). In order to restore the normal sequence, the starred base must be deleted: *UGA* GGU CCU C→UGG GUC CUC*...

Chapter 11 Answers

1.

Strain	-lac	+lac
1	−	−
2	−	−
3	+	+
4	−	−
5	−	−
6	−	−

Strain 1 has a defective *z* gene, and will never make *z*. Strain 2 will never make RNA. Strain 3 makes a nonfunctional repressor, and hence the operon is always on. In strains 4–6, we must look at one DNA at a time (concept 11-D). In strain 4, the first DNA will never make RNA (concept 11-A); the second DNA will never make *z* (concept 11-C). In strain 5, no RNA is made from the first DNA *(p–)*; no *z* product is made from the second DNA. In strain 6, the first DNA always yields a nonfunctional *z*, and a repressor that can't bind lactose. This repressor will bind to both DNAs (concept 11-B) and turn off the bottom DNA permanently.

2. *b* = gene, *a* = operator, *c* = repressor. Look first for the single mutation that never produces enzyme; this genotype will give the letter of the structural gene. The genotype $a^+b^-c^+$ fits this requirement (concept 11-C), so *b* is the structural gene and *a,c* represent control regions. Genotype 4 tells us nothing. Look at genotype 7. The second DNA will never make the enzyme (concept 11-C and 11-D). If *a* is the repressor, the good repressor from the second DNA should bind to the good promoter of the first DNA, and the production of the enzyme should only occur in the presence of lactose (concept 11-C). This is not seen, so *a* must be the operator. If *a* is the operator, the first DNA should always be on, and the enzyme should always be produced (concept 11-A).

3. $i^- o^c z^- y^+/i^+ o^+ z^+ y^-$. To produce β-galactosidase by induction, one DNA must have a normal operator and *z* gene (concept 11-A). At least one DNA must produce a normal repressor so it can bind to o^+ (concept 11-B). Let this i^+ be on the same DNA as above; therefore $i^+ o^+ z^+$. This DNA must be y^-, or else permease production would have been inducible (concept 11-C). This entire DNA is $i^+ o^+ z^+ y^-$. In order to make only permease constitutively, the other DNA must be $z^- y^+$, and the operator must not be able to bind the repressor, o^c (concepts 11-A and 11-C). Since we already have a good *i* gene on the other DNA, the *i* gene can be either i^+ or i^-. Let it be i^-; so this DNA is $i^- o^c z^- y^+$.

4. a. $i^- o^+ z^+$ or $i^+ o^c z^+$

b. inducible for case 1, constitutive for case 2.

For the operon to be always on, the repressor must not be able to bind to the operator. This could occur if the repressor were defective (i^-) or the operator could not bind the repressor (o^c) (concepts 11-A and 11-B). Thus the strain could be either $i^+ o^c z^+$ or $i^- o^+ z^+$. Now set each possible strain up as a partial diploid: $i^+ o^c z^+/i^+ o^+ z^+$ and $i^- o^+ z^+/i^+ o^+ z^+$. In the first case, repressor from neither DNA can bind o^c, and enzyme synthesis is constitutive. In the second case, a good repressor from wild-type DNA will bind to both operators, and the synthesis of the enzyme will be inducible (concepts 11-B and 11-D).

5. **a.** *P, Q* = structural genes, *R, S* = regulators.

   b. Enzyme 1 is inducible in both cases; enzyme 2 is inducible in case 1, and constitutive in case 2.

   Since P^- and Q^- each fail to make enzymes, they must be structural genes (concept 11-C), and *P* = gene 2 and *Q* = gene 1. Since R^- fails to produce either enzyme, it is most likely the promoter. Since S^- always makes enzymes, the repressor is probably not able to bind the operator, so *S* = operator (concept 11-D). In 1, the first DNA will never make enzyme 1 *(Q^-)*, but will make enzyme 2 inducibly. The second DNA will never make enzyme 2 *(P^-)*, but will make enzyme 1 inducibly (concept 11-D). In 2, the second DNA will never make enzyme 1 but will make enzyme 2 constitutively *(S^-)*. The first DNA will never make enzyme 2, but will make enzyme 1 by induction.

6. Almost all transcripts will be full-length operon RNA; little attenuation will occur. In order to make shortened, attenuated RNA, charged tRNA^{trp} must be able to bind to *trp* codons in the attenuator. Since *UGG* is the codon for tryptophan, charged tRNA^{trp} will not recognize *AGG* (concept 11-F). As tryptophan begins to be made, it will bind to the repressor and activate it so it can bind to the operator (concepts 11-C and 11-E).

7. There are probably two enhancers, one located downstream and another located upstream of the gene. A reduction in overall mRNA made suggests that an enhancer sequence has been altered. Enhancers can be found on either side of a gene, and can exert their effect over large distances (concept 11-G).

8. **a.** no enzymes made; *cis* dominant.

   b. enzymes always made; not *cis* dominant if a defect in the repressor, but *cis* dominant if a defect in the operator.

   c. enzymes always made, not *cis* dominant.

   In order for transcription to occur, the promoter must be functional. A defect in a promoter will always affect only the DNA on which it is located (concept 11-A). In (b), either the repressor is defective or the operator is defective. A defective repressor can be overcome by a good repressor from another DNA (*trans* acting) (concept 11-B). In order to bind the operator, the repressor must first combine with a co-repressor (concept 11-E).

9. Liver DNA for the gene is transcribed into an RNA with four introns that are removed, and hence will not hybridize to the DNA. In bone marrow, the splicing is different. The second intron from the liver appears to still be present in the bone marrow RNA, as does part of the third intron (concept 11-I).

10. Operator between *B* and *C;* promoter between *D* and *E*. Promoter mutations will never make RNA (concept 11-A), and we see this result with strains 4 and 5. They both share a deletion of the region between *D* and *E*. Operator mutations usually cannot bind repressors, and enzyme production is constitutive. Strains 2 and 3 show this behavior, and both strains are missing the region *B*. Thus *B* is probably the operator.

11. Gene *A:* transcribed in neurula and bone marrow. Gene *B:* transcribed from fertilization to gastrula, and in adult liver. If a gene cannot be detected after DNase I

treatment, it is probably active transcriptionally. We match the minuses with stages to determine when each gene is active (concept 11-H).

12. Removal of introns did not occur. If a mature RNA had its introns removed, loops should have been seen. The removal of introns is necessary for proper translation of RNA (concept 11-I).

13. Isolate insulin mRNA from a normal individual and hybridize it to DNA from a diabetic. If the promoter is defective, the gene will still be present and should hybridize to the RNA. If the gene is missing, no hybridization will occur (concepts 11-A and 11-C).

Chapter 12 Answers

1. *B* has more *G-C* pairs. Since each *G-C* pair has three hydrogen bonds, it requires more energy to be broken (concept 12-B).

2. Single-stranded. In a double-stranded molecule *A = T* and *G = C*. These ratios are not seen for this molecule (concept 12-A).

3. 1: DS DNA; 2: SS DNA; 3: SS RNA; 4: DS RNA. Look first to see if *T* or *U* is present; this will determine if the molecule is DNA or RNA. Now look to see if *A = T (U)* and *G = C* to determine if it is double- or single-stranded. Molecules 1 and 4 are double-stranded (concept 12-A).

4. **a.** *5′ T T G G T C G A T G T A A T C A T C G C C 3′*

   b. *5′ G G C G A U G A U U A C A U C G A C C A A 3′*

   c. *met-ile-thr-ser*

   Read the sequence directly from the bottom up, and remember that the 5′ end is at the bottom. If a band appears in both *C* and *C+T*, it is *C*. If it appears in both *A* and *A+G*, it is *A* (concept 12-L). Remember that RNA is transcribed in a 5′ to 3′ direction, and that nucleic acids are anti-parallel. To determine the amino acid sequence, find the first *AUG* moving 5′ to 3′ and then block off successive triplets (see chapter 10).

5. 1, 4, 8, and 12 bases.

   The dideoxy method makes a complementary sequence; fragments will appear where *ddC* will be incorporated, beginning with the 5′ end of the newly synthesized strand (concept 12-L).

6.
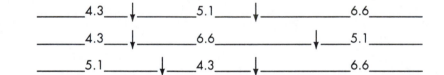

   There are three fragments, so there must be two sites (concept 12-D). Any one of the three fragments could be in the middle. Without any reference point, an order of

   is the same as the answer above.

7. **a.** 4.9, 1.2

   b. 2.1, 0.6, 2.2, 1.2

   If a site is lost, no digestion can occur and we see a new, larger fragment (concept 12-E). A mutation that creates a new site will eliminate one fragment, and create two new fragments that are smaller than the "lost" fragment (concept 12-F).

8. **a.** Yes.

   b. No.

Since Huntington's disease is inherited in a dominant manner, it is likely that any individual with the trait will be heterozygous, and hence produce fragments both from the normal gene and the mutant gene. The husband's pattern represents the normal gene. When we compare this pattern with the woman's father, we see two new bands that result from the creation of a new site within the top normal fragment (concept 12-F). The third and fifth bands should contain DNA from both the normal and mutant genes. The woman's pattern is identical to her father, so she is also heterozygous. The fetus is normal. Thus we can draw the DNA of her father as

9. **b and c.** Begin with the digest from enzyme *B*. Three orders are possible: 1.5, 4.0, 3.5; or 1.5, 3.5, 4.0; or 3.5, 1.5, 4.0. The 1.1 and 2.7 fragments appear in both *A* and mixed digests. Therefore, these pieces do not contain a *B* site (concept 12-G). Since none of the *B* fragments appear in the mix, each *B* fragment must contain an *A* site (concept 12-G). Assume order (b) is correct. This order should produce 2.0 and 1.5 fragments from the right side of the molecule (concept 12-H). These fragments are not seen, so order (b) is not correct. Now assume (c) is correct. This order predicts fragments of 1.1 and 0.4 from the left end of the molecule, and 0.8 and 2.7 from the right end. This result is also not seen, so (a) is the correct map.

10. **a.** circular.

   b.

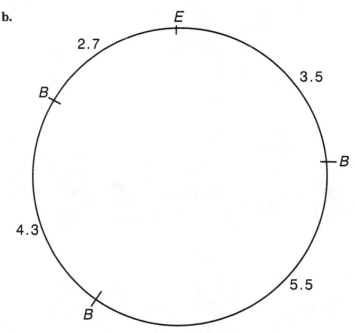

The molecule is either a circle, or has no *EcoRI* site (concepts 12-C and 12-D). If there are no sites, we should see the same fragments in both the *BglII* digest and the mix. The 4.3 and 5.5 kb fragments appear in both *BglII* and the mix. Therefore, the 6.2 kb fragment contains an *EcoRI* site (concepts 12-G and 12-H). The positions of the 3.5 and 2.7 kb fragments and the 4.3 and 5.5 kb fragments could be reversed.

11. 1.5 and 2.7 kb. The inserted gene can be removed from the plasmid by *EcoRI* to yield a 4.2 kb fragment. Since the double digest lacks this fragment, it must contain a *HindIII* site (concept 12-G). Now look for two or more fragments that add up to 4.2 (concept 12-H); these are 1.5 and 2.7.

12. a. The 6.0 and 14.0 kb molecules are dimers of the gene and plasmid respectively.

    b. 10 kb.

    When molecules are mixed and ligated, sometimes dimers are formed as well as original molecules. The 3.0 and 7.0 kb molecules are monomers of the gene and plasmid, and the 14 and 6 kb molecules are dimers. Only the 10 kb piece is the desired one.

13. a.

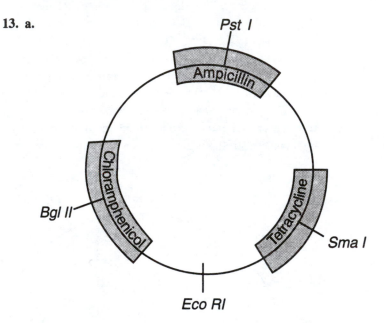

b.

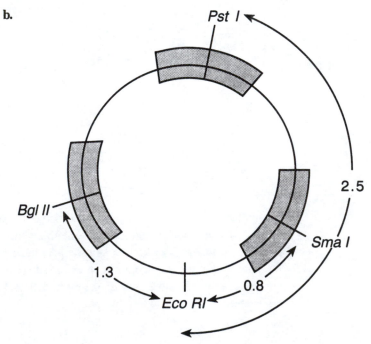

Since the hybrid molecule maintains resistance to all antibiotics when DNA is inserted into the *EcoRI* site, this site does not lie within any of the three genes; it could be anywhere outside of the genes. If resistance is lost, the insertion site is within the gene (concepts 12-I and 12-J). Since the mixes of *EcoRI* and *BglII* or *EcoRI* + *SmaI* yield a fragment less than that produced by *EcoRI* + *PstI*, the *EcoRI* site must be between tetracycline and chloramphenicol. The rest of the positions can be determined by adding fragments (concept 12-H).

14.

$$
\begin{array}{ccccc}
 & H & & H & \\
3.0 & \downarrow & 4.0 & \downarrow & 5.0
\end{array}
$$

$$
\begin{array}{ccccc}
1.8 & \updownarrow & 2.7 & \updownarrow & 5.3 & \updownarrow & 2.2 \\
 & B & & B & & B
\end{array}
$$

Remember that a DNA molecule will be labeled at each end, since it is double-stranded. The single digests indicate the following sequences:

HindIII:	3.0* ↓	4.0	↓	5.0*	
BglII:	1.8* ↓	(2.2, 5.3)	↓	2.2*	or
	2.2* ↓	(2.2, 5.3)	↓	1.8*	

(concept 12-D). If the second *BglII* order is correct, the mix should produce a 0.8 kb fragment, and this is not seen. Therefore, we now have:

HindIII:	3.0* ↓	4.0	↓	5.0*
BglII:	1.8* ↓	(2.2, 5.3)	↓	2.2*

If the 5.3 kb fragment is next to 1.8, we expect fragments of 0.1 and 3.1 kb which are not seen. If the 2.7 kb fragment is next to 1.8, we expect to see a 1.5 kb fragment (concepts 12-G and 12-H).

15. Embryonic DNA has lost restriction site(s) and formed new ones during development. The cDNA will bind to those fragments that contain sequences for the antibody gene (concept 12-K). Since new fragments appear, old sites have been lost and new ones generated, possibly by moving regions of DNA (concepts 12-E and 12-F).

Chapter 13 Answers

1. $M = 0.43$; $N = 0.57$. No, it is not in equilibrium. Calculate the frequency of M and N alleles as:

$$M = [300 + \frac{1}{2}(180)]/900 = {}^{390}\!/_{900} = 0.43$$
$$N = [420 + \frac{1}{2}(180)]/900 = {}^{510}\!/_{900} = 0.57 \qquad \text{(concept 13-A)}$$

   If the population is in equilibrium, we expect the frequency of MM individuals to be $(0.43)^2 = 0.18$; of MN to be $2 \times (0.43)(0.57) = 0.49$, and NN to be $(0.57)^2 = 0.33$ (concept 13-B). The observed frequencies are ${}^{300}\!/_{900} = 0.33\ MM$, ${}^{180}\!/_{900} = 0.2\ MN$, and ${}^{420}\!/_{900} = 0.47\ NN$.

2. $0.18\ MM$, $0.49\ MN$, $0.33\ NN$. In the absence of external forces, equilibrium will be achieved within one generation. Thus, the expected frequencies calculated in problem one apply (concept 13-B).

3. $I^A = 0.05\ I^B = 0.15$; $I^O = 0.8$. Since we have three alleles, the distribution can be calculated as $(p + q + r)^2 = 1$. In this equation, we can let r^2 = frequency of type O individuals = ${}^{128}\!/_{200}$ (concept 13-E). So $r = 0.8$. If p = frequency of I^A, then $(p + r)^2$ = frequency of type A + frequency of type O = $0.085 + 0.64 = 0.725$. Therefore $(p + 0.8)^2 = 0.725$ and $p = 0.05$. Since $p + q + r = 1.0$, and since $p + r = 0.85$, q = frequency of $I^B = 0.15$.

4. 0.25. First calculate allele frequencies.

$$M = [69 + \frac{1}{2}(108)]/300 = 69 + {}^{54}\!/_{300} = {}^{123}\!/_{300} = 0.41 \qquad \text{(concept 13-A)}$$
$$N = 1 - 0.41 = 0.59 \qquad \text{(concept 13-A)}$$

   Now calculate the observed frequency of heterozygotes:

$$ {}^{108}\!/_{300} = 0.36 $$

   and expected frequency of heterozygotes:

$$2\ pq = 2\ (0.41)(0.59) = 0.48 \text{ (concept 13-B)}$$

   Inbreeding coefficient,

$$f = 1 - (\text{observed/expected}) = 1 - (0.36/0.48) = 1 - 0.75 = 0.25 \qquad \text{(concept 13-H)}$$

5. **a.** $p = 0.2$, $q = 0.8$

   b. $p = 0.08$, $q = 0.92$

   We need to set up an equation that satisfies the information:

$$q^2 = 2\ (2\ pq) = 4\ pq$$

   Substitute $1 - q$ for p (concept 13-A).

$$q^2 = 4\ q\ (1 - q) = 4\ q - 4\ q^2$$
$$0 = 4\ q - 5\ q^2$$
$$0 = q\ (4 - 5\ q)$$
$$\text{either } q = 0 \text{ or } 5q = 4$$

   q cannot equal 0, or there would be no homozygous recessives. So, q must equal 0.8. Check by substituting into the Hardy-Weinberg equation:

$$q^2 = 0.64,\ 2\ pq = 2\ (0.2)(0.8) = 0.32 \qquad \text{(concept 13-B)}$$

Similar logic is used for part (b):

$$q^2 = 6 (2\ pq) = 12\ pq = 12\ q - 12\ q^2$$
$$0 = q (12 - 13q)\ q = 0\ (\text{impossible})\ \text{or}\ q = {}^{12}\!/_{13} = 0.92$$

Check again by substituting:

$$q^2 = (0.92)^2 = 0.846,\ 2\ pq = 2\ (0.08)\ (0.92) = 0.14 \qquad (\text{concept 13-B})$$

6. a. 0.007

b. 1.4

Since cystic fibrosis results from a recessive allele, the frequency of the allele is:

$$\sqrt{\text{frequency of phenotype}} = \sqrt{1/20,000} = \sqrt{0.00005} = 0.007\ (\text{concept 13–C})$$

q and $p = 1 - q = 0.993$.

The expected frequency of carriers is

$$2\ pq = 2\ (0.993)\ (0.007) = .014 \qquad (\text{concept 13-B})$$

7. a. $p = 0.92,\ q = 0.08$

b. 0.92

Since a woman needs two copies of a recessive allele to show the phenotype, the frequency of women with the disease is q^2. Therefore $q = \sqrt{64/10,000} = 0.08$ (concept 13-C). Therefore $p = 1 - q = 0.92$. Since males have only one X chromosome, the expected frequency of color-blind males is q, or 0.08 (concept 13-D). Therefore, 0.92 of males should be normal.

8. a. 0.01

b. .0198, or about 2%

The frequency of the recessive allele is the same as affected males, or 0.01 (concept 13-D). Therefore, $p = 1 - p = 0.99$. Frequency of heterozygotes is $2pq = 2 (0.01) (0.99) = 0.0198$ (concept 13-B).

9. 0.704 $A_1 A_1$; 0.192 $A_1 A_2$; 0.104 $A_2 A_2$. We use the relationship in concept 13-G:

$$A_1 A_1 = p^2 + fpq = (0.8)^2 + (0.4)\ (0.8)\ (0.2) = 0.704$$
$$A_2 A_2 = q^2 + fpq = (0.2)^2 + (0.4)\ (0.8)\ (0.2) = 0.104$$
$$A_1 A_2 = 2\ pq - 2\ fpq = 2\ (0.8)\ (0.2) - 2\ (0.4)\ (0.8)\ (0.2) = 0.32 - 0.128 = 0.192$$

10. 0.48 A; 0.15 B; 0.36 AB; 0.01 O. Since the population is in equilibrium, the genotypic frequencies can be calculated as:

$$(p + q + r)^2 = p^2 + 2\ pq + q^2 + 2\ qr + r^2 \qquad (\text{concept 13-E})$$

Let $p = 0.6$, $q = 0.3$, and $r = 0.1$. Blood types will be represented by the following:

A: $p^2 + 2\ pr$	B: $q^2 + 2\ qr$	AB: $2\ pq$	O: r^2
= 0.36 + 0.12	= 0.09 + 0.06	= 0.36	= 0.01

11. 0.375. First calculate expected heterozygote frequency as:

$$2\,pq = 2\,(0.8)\,(0.2) = 0.32 \quad \text{(concept 13-B)}$$

The inbreeding coefficient is:

$$1 - (\text{observed/expected}) = 1 - (.20/.32) = 1 - 0.625 = 0.375 \quad \text{(concept 13-H)}$$

12. Attack. The expected frequency of yellow seeds will depend on the allele frequencies of the original population. If we assume that mating is random with respect to seed color, and there is no selection, we can calculate the frequencies of yellow seeds for two different populations at equilibrium (concept 13-B). Let p = frequency of yellow allele, and q = frequency of green allele.

Population	p	q	Frequency of yellow ($p^2 + 2\,pq$)
1	0.7	0.3	0.91
2	0.5	0.5	0.75

We see that the original premise will be met only if initially the alleles are equally frequent.

13. $C^B = 0.273$; $C^P = 0.467$; $C^Y = 0.26$

We first must assign genotypes to each color:

$$\text{Brown:} \quad C^B C^B,\ C^B C^P,\ C^B C^Y$$
$$\text{Pink:} \quad C^P C^P,\ C^P C^Y$$
$$\text{Yellow:} \quad C^Y C^Y$$

Let p = frequency of C^B, q = frequency of C^P, and r = frequency of C^Y.

Now calculate frequencies of each color:

$$\text{Brown:} \quad {}^{472}\!/_{1000} = 0.472$$
$$\text{Pink:} \quad {}^{462}\!/_{1000} = 0.462$$
$$\text{Yellow:} \quad {}^{66}\!/_{1000} = 0.066$$

The frequency of yellow is r^2 (concept 13-E), so $r = \sqrt{0.066} = 0.26$ (concept 13-C).

$$\text{Frequency of yellow + frequency of pink} = (q + r)^2 \quad \text{(concept 13-E)}$$
$$(q + r)^2 = 0.528$$
$$q + r = \sqrt{0.528} = 0.727$$
$$q = 0.727 - r = 0.727 - 0.26 = 0.467$$
$$\text{Now, } p + q + r = 1.0, \text{ so } p + 0.727 = 1, \text{ and } p = 1 - 0.727 = 0.273.$$

14. a. $M = 0.652$, $N = 0.348$

 b. No.

 c. $f = 0.267$

Calculate frequency of M as:

$$0.486 + \tfrac{1}{2} (0.332) = 0.652$$

and frequency of N as:

$$0.182 + \tfrac{1}{2} (0.332) = 0.348 \qquad \text{(concept 13-A)}$$

Calculate expected heterozygote frequency as:

$$2\,pq = 2\,(0.652)\,(0.348) = 0.453 \qquad \text{(concept 13-B)}$$

Since there is a reduction in observed heterozygotes, the population is not at equilibrium (concept 13-B). The expected frequency of NN is: $(0.348)^2 = 0.121$. We see an increase in homozygous NN individuals, so inbreeding must be occurring (concept 13-F). The inbreeding coefficient is:

$$1 - (0.332/0.454) = 1 - 0.731 = 0.269 \qquad \text{(concept 13-H)}$$

Chapter 14 Answers

1. 3000. Since initially there are no resistant cells, there is no reverse mutation rate. Thus the frequency of resistant cells will be $p\mu$ or (10^{11}) $(3 \times 10^{-8}) = 3 \times 10^3$ (concept 14-A).

2. **a.** $p = 0.67997$, $q = 0.32003$

   b. $\hat{p} = 0.05$, $\hat{q} = 0.95$

   c. 0.02

   Since $q = 0.32$, $p = 0.68$, we can calculate the change in q after one generation.

   $$\Delta q = \mu p - vq = (2 \times 10^{-5})\,(6.8 \times 10^{-1}) - (10^{-6})\,(3.2 \times 10^{-1}) =$$
   $$(136 \times 10^{-7}) - (3.2 \times 10^{-7}) = 132.8 \times 10^{-7} = 1.33 \times 10^{-5}$$

   Therefore $q_1 = 0.32003$ and $p_1 = 0.67997$ (concept 14-B). We now calculate equilibrium frequencies.

   $$\hat{q} = \mu/(\mu + v) = (2 \times 10^{-5})/(2.1 \times 10^{-5}) = 0.95$$
   $$\hat{p} = (1 \times 10^{-6})/(2.1 \times 10^{-5}) = 0.05 \qquad \text{(concept 14-C)}$$

   Since both mutation and selection are operating, we use the relationship

   $$\hat{q} = \sqrt{\mu/s} = \sqrt{\left(2 \times 10^{-5}\right)/10^{-1}} = \sqrt{2 \times 10^{-4}} = 2 \times 10^{-2} = 0.02 \quad \text{(concept 14-J)}$$

   Recall that selection = 1 − fitness.

3. 0.83; 0.91; 0.67. Since the only factor changing allele frequencies is mutation, we use the equation:

   $$\hat{q} = \mu/(\mu + v) \qquad \text{(concept 14-C)}$$

   In the first case,

   $$\mu = 5v, \text{ so } \hat{q} = 5v/(5v + v) = \tfrac{5}{6} = 0.83$$

   In the second case,

   $$\mu = 10v, \text{ so } \hat{q} = 10v/(10v + v) = \tfrac{10}{11} = 0.91$$

   In the third case,

   $$\mu = 2v, \text{ so } \hat{q} = 2v/(2v + v) = \tfrac{2}{3} = 0.67$$

4. 0.219. We use the relationship $m = (q - q')/(q - q_m)$ where q = frequency in the native population, q' = frequency in the mixed population, and q_m = frequency in the migrant population (concept 14-E). Substituting, we get

   $$m = (0 - 0.094)/(0 - 0.429) = 0.219$$

5. 0.32. We must first calculate allele frequencies in each population. Recall that $q = \sqrt{\text{frequency of blue-eyed individuals}}$ (see chapter 13). $q_m = \sqrt{0.16} = 0.4$ and $q = \sqrt{0.09} = 0.3$. Now we use the relationship:

   $$q' = q - m\,(q - q_m) \text{ (concept 14-D)} = 0.3 - 0.2\,(0.3 - 0.4) = 0.3 + 0.02 = 0.32$$

6. 0.478 *AA*; 0.378 *Aa*; 0.144 *aa*; $p = 0.67$, $q = 0.33$. After random mating, the frequencies will be the product of the original frequency and the fitness (concept 14-F).

Therefore,

$$AA = 1 \ (0.33) = 0.33$$
$$Aa = (0.8) \ (0.33) = 0.26$$
$$aa = (0.3) \ (0.33) = 0.1$$

The relative frequency of each genotype is then:

$$AA = 0.33/0.69 = 0.478$$
$$Aa = 0.26/0.69 = 0.378$$
$$aa = 0.1/0.69 = 0.144$$

Since p = freq AA + ½ freq Aa (chapter 13), $p = 0.478 + ½ \ (0.378) = 0.67$. Since $q = 1 - p$, $q = 0.33$.

7. 0.58. Let s_1 = selection coefficient of Tf^A/Tf^A and s_2 = selection coefficient Tf^B/Tf^B. Therefore,

$$\hat{q} \ (Tf^B) = 0.31/(0.31 \times 0.22) = 0.31/0.53 = 0.58 \qquad \text{(concept 14-I)}$$

In most pigeon populations the frequency of Tf^B ranges from 0.55 to 0.59.

8. 0.174; 0.154. Since we are concerned with the allele frequencies one and two generations after selection, we use the relationship:

$$q_s = q \ (1 - sq)/(1 - sq^2) \quad \text{(concept 14-G)}$$

After one generation,

$$\begin{aligned} q_1 &= 0.2 \ [1 - (0.2) \ (0.8)]/[1 - (0.8) \ (0.04)] \\ &= 0.2 \ (1 - 0.16)/(1 - 0.032) \\ &= (0.2) \ (0.84)/0.968 \\ &= 0.174 \end{aligned}$$

In the second generation, the starting frequency is 0.174. It is easier to rewrite the equation as

$$\begin{aligned} q_s &= (q - sq^2)/1 - sq^2 \\ &= [0.174 - (0.8) \ (0.174)^2]/[1 - (0.8) \ (0.174)^2] \\ &= 0.150/0.976 \\ &= 0.154 \end{aligned}$$

9. 0.528. Let $q_m = 0.25$, $q' = 0.5$, and $m = 0.1$. Set up the equation

$$m = (q - q')/(q - q_m) \qquad \text{(concept 14-E)}$$

Rearrange so $m \ (q - q_m) = q - q'$ or $q = mq - mq_m + q'$

$$q - mq = q' - mq_m \text{ or } q \ (1 - m) = q' - mq_m$$
$$\begin{aligned} q &= (q' - mq_m)/(1 - m) \\ &= [0.5 - (0.1) \ (0.25)]/0.9 \\ &= (0.5 - 0.025)/0.9 \\ &= 0.475/0.9 \\ &= 0.528 \end{aligned}$$

10. 0.012. Since both mutation and selection are operating,

$$\hat{q} = \sqrt{\mu/s} \text{ (concept 14 - J). Let } \mu = 3 \times 10^{-5} \text{ and } s = 0.2$$

$$\hat{q} = \sqrt{\left(3 \times 10^{-5}\right)/0.2} = \sqrt{1.5 \times 10^{-4}} = 1.22 \times 10^{-2} = .012$$

11. 6×10^{-5}. Since we are dealing with a dominant mutation, the equilibrium frequency is: mutation rate/selection coefficient (concept 14-J). Since fitness = 0.25, $s = 0.75$ and $\mu = 4.5 \times 10^{-5}$.

$$\hat{q} = 4.5 \times 10^{-5}/0.75 = 0.6 \times 10^{-4}$$

12. $0.476\ B_1B_1;\ 0.428\ B_1B_2;\ 0.096\ B_1B_2$. We simply use concept 14-G:

$$
\begin{aligned}
q_s &= (q - sq^2)/(1 - sq^2) \\
&= [0.4 - (0.8)(0.16)]/[1 - (0.8)(0.16)] \\
&= (0.4 - 0.128)/(1 - 0.128) \\
&= 0.272/0.872 \\
&= 0.31 \\
\text{and } p &= 0.69
\end{aligned}
$$

These genotypes will be distributed as:

$$
\begin{aligned}
p^2\ B_1\ B_1 &= (0.69)^2 = 0.476 \\
2\ pq\ B_1\ B_2 &= 2\ (0.31)\ (0.69) = 0.428 \\
q^2\ B_2\ B_2 &= (0.31)^2 = 0.096
\end{aligned}
$$

13. frequency of $r = 0.337$; frequency of $s = 0.663$. First, calculate selection coefficients as: 1 − fitness. s_1 = selection coefficient of normal homozygote = 1 − 0.68 = 0.32, and s_2 = selection coefficient of homozygous mutant = 1 − 0.37 = 0.63. Therefore,

$$\hat{q} = 0.32/(0.32 + 0.63) = 0.32/0.95 = 0.337 \qquad \text{(concept 14-I)}$$

Since $p + q = 1$, $\hat{p} = 1 - 0.337$ (see chapter 13).

14. 1.4×10^{-6}. Since very few individuals are affected, the frequency of the recessive, normal allele is just about one, and the homozygous dominant is expected to be nonexistent. Therefore all affected individuals are heterozygous, or $2\ pq = 4 \times 10^{-6}$. Since $q \approx 1$, $2p = 4 \times 10^{-6}$, or $p = 2 \times 10^{-6}$. We assume this value is an equilibrium value, so $\hat{p} = \mu/s$ (concept 14-J), or $(\hat{p})\ (s) = \mu$.

$$(2 \times 10^{-6})(0.7) = 1.4 \times 10^{-6}$$

15. 0.078. First determine if population is in equilibrium by calculating allele frequencies and computing expected genotypic frequencies.

$$q = 0.000064 + \tfrac{1}{2}\ (0.015872) = 0.008 \text{ and } p = 0.992 \text{ (see chapter 13)}$$

We expect $(8 \times 10^{-3})^2 = 0.000064\ aa$ and $(0.992)^2 = 0.984064\ AA$. Therefore this population is in equilibrium (see chapter 13) and

$$\hat{q}^2 = \mu/s \text{ or } s = \mu/\hat{q}^2 = 5 \times 10^{-6}/64 \times 10^{-6} = 0.078 \qquad \text{(concept 14-J)}$$

16. 0.0099; 0.0098. Since the homozygote is lethal, $s = 1$. Therefore,

$$q_1 = q/(1 + q) \text{ (concept 14-H)} = 0.01/1.01 = 0.0099$$

For the second generation we start with $q = 0.0099$, so $q_2 = 0.0099/1.0099 = 0.0098$. This situation is typical of many recessive human disorders such as Tay-Sachs or cystic fibrosis.

Chapter 15 Answers

1. **a.** 3 red : 3 vermillion : 1 brown : 1 white

    b. 9 red : 3 vermillion : 3 brown : 1 white

    c. 2 red : 1 vermillion : 1 brown

    d. 2 red : 1 vermillion : 1 brown

    In each cross, diagram the original cross and the $F_1 \times F_1$. Remember that there is no crossing over in *Drosophila* males, and that genes 50 or more map units apart behave as if they are unlinked (see chapters 1, 2, 4, and 5).

2. A-2; B-1; C-4; D-3. White can be either X^w and any other gene, or *cn cn; se se*. Cross 2 must be:

    $$se/se; ++ \times ++; cn/cn,$$

    which will give a 9:3:3:1 ratio. Cross 2 goes with vial A. In cross 1, sepia male must be X^+Y; *se/se*. If the female in cross 1 is $X^wX^w;+/+$, the cross of the F_1s is:

    $$X^+X^w; +/se \times X^wY; +/se$$

    which yields:

3 $X^+-; +-$	red
3 $X^W-; +-$	white
1 $X^+-; se/se$	sepia
1 $X^W-; se/se$	white

    Vial C gives different results for the sexes so X^w must be involved. The F_2 females show the ratio expected for two autosomal genes, so they must be X^+. The original cross is then:

    $$X^+X^+; cn/cn; se/se \times X^+Y; +/+; +/+$$

    In D, we see a ratio that suggests one autosomal gene is heterozygous in the F_1s. The male must be *cn/cn; se/se* and the female is *cn/cn;+/+* (see chapters 1, 2, and 4).

3. **a.** all wire hair.

    b. all wire hair.

    Homozygous hairless must be lethal, and hairless must be dominant. We have three alleles with a peck order dominance: hairless > wire > straight (see chapter 1).

4. **a.** $\frac{9}{48}$

    b. $\frac{1}{4}$

    To produce gold, an individual must be +/–, +/–, and *fe/fe* for tin, mercury, and iron, respectively. Therefore,

    $$\frac{3}{4} \times \frac{3}{4} \times \frac{1}{3} = \frac{9}{48}$$

    (We use $\frac{1}{3}$ since only $\frac{3}{4}$ of all genotypes survive and $\frac{2}{3}$ of these will be *Fe/fe*.) In (b), $\frac{1}{4}$ of everyone will be *sn/sn*, and hence tin (see chapters 1 and 2).

5. ____ *j* _____ 32.2 ___ *ct* __ 4.5 __ *fa* _____ >50 ____ *ba* ___

Balloon can be on either end. Cross A shows that all four genes are recessive. Cross B shows that all four genes are linked. Remember that there is no crossing over in *Drosophila* males. In cross C, we see four majority classes, indicating that one gene is assorting independently of the others. Comparing *j* and *fa*, we see only two classes, so *j* and *fa* are linked. When we compare *fa* and *ba*, we see four classes, so *ba* is > 50 m.u. from the other genes. Ignoring balloon, we can map *j*, *fa*, and *ct* (see chapters 1 and 5).

6. all wild females

males:	397	*m + scr*
	78	*m + +*
	23	*+ + scr*
	2	*+ + +*

The heterozygous female is *m + scr/+ l +*. Calculate the observed dco as

$$(0.5)(0.05)(0.16) = 0.004$$

Now calculate expected frequencies for all eight classes. Those classes with *l* will die (see chapters 1, 4, and 5).

7. a. autosomal recessive.

b. autosomal recessive.

c. two different genes.

Since two normal individuals produce mutant progeny, the trait is recessive. If it were X-linked, only ½ of the males should be affected. The fact that two affected individuals produce all normal children indicates that we are dealing with two genes (see chapters 2 and 6).

8. a. *lys$^+$ his$^+$ val$^+$*
    lys$^+$ his$^+$ val$^-$
    lys$^+$ his$^-$ val$^+$
    lys$^+$ his$^-$ val$^-$

    Lys$^+$ must be present to allow growth.

b. *lys$^+$ val$^+$ his$^+$*
    lys$^+$ val$^+$ his$^-$

    Lys$^+$ and *val$^+$* must be present to allow growth.

c. *lys$^+$ val$^+$ his$^+$*
    lys$^+$ val$^-$ his$^+$

    Lys$^+$ and *his$^+$* must be present to allow growth.

d. *lys$^+$ val$^+$ his$^-$*
    lys$^+$ val$^-$ his$^+$

    We see no *lys$^+$ val$^+$ his$^+$*.

    e. *lys⁺* and *val⁺* are close together; they are co-transformed 75 percent of the time. The order could be *lys val his* or *val lys his*.

    f. *val lys his.* If the order is *val lys his*, *val⁺ lys⁻ his⁺* should be rare, since this genotype results from a double exchange (see chapter 9).

9.

	-*lac*	+*lac*
A	+	+
B	–	–
C	–	+
D	–	+
E	–	+
F	–	–

(see chapter 11)

10. Q = operator and T = promoter. Operator mutations will always be on, so deletion 1, covering Q, contains the operator. A promoter mutation, or a defect in one of the two structural genes, will never make silk. So 2, 3, or 4 (R, S, or T) could be promoter. Among the diploids, if R = promoter, strain 2 should have normal control sequences and hence be inducible, since S and T should complement each other. Thus R is not the promoter. In strain 3, if S = promoter, the first DNA is never on and the second DNA should be inducible but makes defective R. T must be the promoter (see chapters 9 and 11).

11. $e = z$; $y = i$; $u = o$; $r = p$. Strains with mutations in either p or z should never give activity (e, r). Operator and repressor mutants should always give some activity (u, y). A $z⁻/z⁻$ and $z⁻/p⁻$ should never give activity, so we can't really distinguish between $z⁻$ and $p⁻$ mutations from the data. Operator mutations should always give at least 1000 units of activity. Therefore, $u = o⁻$. Mutant y must therefore be $i⁻$ (see chapter 11).

12.

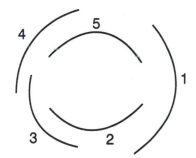

We can't generate a linear map that is consistent with the data. Therefore we try a circle (see chapter 9).

13.

        2 ←— 0.04 —→ 1 ←— 0.02 —→ 3

Plaques on B give the total number of progeny. Plaques on K12 indicate wild-type recombinants, since only wild-type will grow on K12. But this number is only ½ of the recombinants; the other ½ is the double mutant (see chapter 9).

14. **a.** UAA

  b. Olmstead: *CUG* to *CGG;* House: *UAU* to *UAA* or *UAG;*

  Max: *CUGGCC* to *CUG G GCC* (see chapter 10).

15. **a.** Single-stranded; *A* not equal to *T,* and *G* not equal to *C.*

  b. Single-stranded molecules are not expected to melt.

  c. The DNA molecule probably has some complementary regions:

Index